THE TWEETABLE POPE

THE
#TWEETABLE
POPE

• • •

A Spiritual Revolution
in 140 Characters

Michael J. O'Loughlin

First published by HarperCollins in 2015
This edition published by Lion Books
an imprint of
Lion Hudson plc
Wilkinson House, Jordan Hill Road,
Oxford OX2 8DR, England
www.lionhudson.com/lion

ISBN 978 0 7459 6856 8
e-ISBN 978 0 7459 6857 5

Acknowledgments
Pope Benedict photograph by Carlos Alvarez/Getty Images
Pope Francis photograph by Giulio Origlia/Getty Images

Designed by Terry McGrath

A catalogue record for this book is available from the British Library

Printed and bound in the UK, February 2016, LH26

To my mom, dad, and Matt: Thank you.

Contents

1

Tweeting Like a Pope

POPE FRANCIS IS A ROCK STAR. RECORD NUMBERS OF pilgrims fill Saint Peter's Square each week for his general audience. His papal visits attract millions, all hoping for a glimpse of this septuagenarian Argentine dressed in a fraying white cassock. Babies are handed to him and police barricades stand no chance. And oh that swag: Pope Francis bobbleheads, T-shirts, and even plush toys. Everyone wants a piece of this pope. He's been featured on a wide range of magazine covers: *The New Yorker, The Advocate, Fortune, Rolling Stone,* and, of course, *Time,* as their Person of the Year. The media and the public hang on every word, looking for clues about where he intends to lead the Church. Catholics and other Christians, fascinated by Francis, want to know how they might apply some of his lessons to their own lives.

The pope, nearly eighty, has admitted he can't really work a computer. He communicates with his top cardinals via fax machine. And he leads an institution that still uses smoke signals to communicate its most important news. At first glance, Francis may seem like an out-of-date leader for a haplessly ancient institution, at least when it comes to communication. But dig a little deeper, and the key to understanding this fascinating figure and his vision for the Church is found in a decidedly modern place: Twitter.

Using his @Pontifex account, Pope Francis communicates ancient truths, spiritual insights, and bursts of wisdom instantly to his millions of followers. And with the highest re-Tweet rate—followers publishing his messages for their own followers to read—among global leaders, Pope Francis has a platform to spread his spiritual revolution further than any pope before. The pope is able to reach out directly to his people. It's the perfect platform for Francis as he tries to revitalize the Church, one believer at a time.

For those unfamiliar with Twitter, here's a crash course: Twitter is a social network, where users create free profiles to connect with friends and family, as well as journalists, celebrities, politicians, and now even popes. An estimated 300 million users publish thoughts, ideas, or links to websites. Those messages, called Tweets, are limited to 140 characters, and close to 6,000 Tweets are published each second of the day, every day—yes, you read that right: 6,000 per *second*.

Some people dismiss Twitter because of the limit to the number of characters allowed per thought. There can't be much deep thinking going on, they say. But critics miss the point. Figuring out how to distill a complex message down to the essentials, to capture someone's attention in a busy, rushed world, and to convince them to consider how they live their lives is a lot more difficult to do in a few words than it is in an essay or op-ed. But do it well, and you will leave your audience with something powerful to reflect on throughout the day. Do it really well, and you might even change the world.

Still not convinced? Let's take some of Jesus's most powerful teachings. Too deep for Tweets, right? Hardly. "Blessed are the poor in spirit, for theirs is the kingdom of Heaven." At a mere 68 characters, there's still plenty of room for a couple of hashtags. (If you are shaking your head over the term "hashtag," these are what Twitter uses to categorize Tweets and are designated by adding a hashtag [#] in front of a term. So if someone wants to search an established theme or an event, they could search by the hashtag.) For this beatitude, maybe #PoorHereRichThere would work with that little slice of Jesus's sermon.

"Let anyone among you who is without sin be the first to throw a stone at her." Just 77 characters. "I am the way, and the truth, and the life. No one comes to the Father except through me." Only 88 characters. "I give you a new commandment, that you love one another. Just as I have loved you, you also should love one another." At 116, still well below Twitter's maximum of 140 characters. You get the idea. Putting our deepest thoughts into pithy, memorable phrases takes skill, talent, and a deep knowledge of the subject at hand. The rewards can be immeasurable. People remember, reflect, and, hopefully, change their lives in response.

Pope Francis is masterful at this. He's dusting off antiquated parchment and presenting Jesus in a way that's more accessible to the digital generation. His informal but official homilies are known for how they speak to people where they are. He's able to make the seemingly ordinary experiences of everyday life seem graced and meaningful. He does the same on Twitter, connecting with millions around the world, asking them to pause a moment during their hectic lives and consider something deeper. His Tweets connect people to God, by pointing them to moments of grace and showing them the way God calls us each to live. Even limited to 140 characters, the pope's Tweets play a powerful role for his followers.

Speaking of followers, the number of followers someone has is how others assess a leader's influence. As of this book's printing, the worldwide leader for English-language Tweeting is Katy Perry, followed closely by Justin Bieber, with each being followed by more than 75 million people. On that list, Pope Francis comes in far below, well into the triple digits. But Pope

Francis is not limited to English. He Tweets in several languages. His combined total is close to 30 million people. While well shy of pop stars, let's think about that number for a moment. When in history has a pope ever been able to communicate directly to tens of millions of people at a time? Before television, the answer would be never. Even with television, the answer would be very rarely. This pope reaches almost 30 million people, on average, four to five times a week.

The number of followers who re-Tweet the pope's messages means many times the pope's followers read what he has to say, spend some time with it, and maybe even feel a bit closer to God. On Twitter, each follower has the ability to re-Tweet a post to his or her own followers, thus multiplying the reach and impact of a particular Tweet. Since Francis's posts are re-Tweeted at such a high rate, some of his short sermons can reach as many as 200 million people. And the pope's Twitter impact doesn't stop online. Italian news stations use the pope's Tweets in scrolling tickers at the bottom of the screens. English-language media outlets report regularly on the pope's sharpest Tweets, as you will see perhaps most clearly in the chapter on inequality. And I can't even count the number of times friends and colleagues have included in a conversation, "Did you see what the pope Tweeted?"

Surprisingly, Pope Francis has a large number of followers in Saudi Arabia, the United Arab Emirates, and other Gulf states. At first, the Vatican was perplexed. With churches illegal in some of those nations, there aren't a whole lot of Christians in the region. While many Muslims respect Pope Francis, polls show most have no opinion of him. So why the huge following? The pope's Twitter team dug around and realized most of the followers in the Gulf states weren't curious Muslims, but Filipinos who had immigrated to the Middle East to find work.

Many of those workers live grueling lives: corrupt bosses who withhold wages, dangerous and abusive working conditions, and sometimes even outright physical abuse that activists say constitutes modern-day slavery. On top of all that, they sometimes can't practice their faith openly. Even reading a Bible could be dangerous. But rather than lose their faith, they log on to Twitter and follow the pope. It's a way for them to be connected to the Church, their culture, and even a sense of home. So even though Twitter has more than its fair share of mundane celebrity ramblings and trolls intent on spreading hate, it's also a powerful way to practice one's faith, even in the most trying of circumstances. For the Filipino worker stationed in Riyadh, with no church or Christian community, Twitter isn't a distraction or waste of time. It's a tool to connect with the divine.

Since his election in March 2013, Pope Francis has captured the attention—and affection—of the world. Large majorities in Europe (84 percent), the United States (78 percent), and Latin America (72 percent) love the guy, according to a December 2014 poll from the Pew Research Center's Global Attitudes Project. In places where the pope is less well-known, he's still doing pretty well. More than 40 percent of both Africans and Asians have a favorable view of him; a quarter of Middle Easterners are fond of Francis. In the United States, Francis has broken our severe partisan gridlock, appealing to at least 70 percent of both Republicans and Democrats, according to a March 2015 Pew Research Center report. All this popularity has prompted Catholics in the United States to identify more strongly with their faith, and for Catholics in Italy and Ireland, anecdotally at least, to return to Mass. It's also transformed Pope Francis into a veritable social media star, extending his reach in ways previous popes could never have imagined.

Francis inherited Pope Benedict XVI's Twitter handle, @Pontifex, along with 3 million followers. In just a few months, Francis quintupled its reach. Today, among the pope's nine different language accounts, he's amassed close to 30 million followers. And that number grows each day.

Some of the pope's Tweets are what you would expect from the Church's chief cleric: references to Gospel passages, exhortations to prayer and mercy, and a reminder that Christians are called to live life joyfully. Other Tweets, like the pope himself, are more surprising: accolades to sports teams, condolences to people affected by violence, rejoinders about war, economic issues, and even gentle rebukes to those who would prefer this pope not make such a mess of things, as he asked young people to do during a particularly memorable homily. But all Francis's Tweets, as we will see in the following chapters, have one thing in common: moving the Church, meaning the people of God, away from petty distractions and closer to the life and teachings of Jesus.

Putting Francis's Tweets into context helps make sense of a thrilling—if slightly confusing—pope. This might be called the Pendulum Papacy, seemingly hitting the edges of both the ecclesial left and right, sometimes in the same week. As we'll read in the coming pages, Francis slammed conservative Catholics "obsessed" with fighting abortion one day, only to condemn the practice unflinchingly a few days later. His top staffer, speaking for the Holy See, called Ireland's May 2015 decision to legalize same-sex marriage a "defeat for humanity" just weeks before it was reported Francis would meet with a gay activist in South America. This pope prefers simple vestments and liturgy, yet he also appointed a cardinal who champions traditional aspects of the Mass to head the Vatican department concerned with worship. It's understandable that even for his fans, Francis makes heads spin. But there are clues to what this pope has in store for the Church, right there on his Twitter feed. *The Tweetable Pope* examines more than one-third of these Tweets, and will give you the tools to make sense of the rest.

At its heart, the Gospel isn't complicated. And for an older guy intent on revitalizing an institution in crisis and inspiring a troubled world, there's no time for long-windedness. So for Pope Francis, Twitter is the perfect platform. It forces its users to be sharp and to the point, and yet it's capable of moving hearts and minds. Just like the pope himself.

I have a personal stake in writing *The Tweetable Pope*. Back in 2009 when I moved to Washington, DC, people inevitably asked me what I did for work. When I told them I wrote about the Catholic Church, I'd often be greeted with a barrage of complaints, insults, and anger. Some of this seemed justified: gay people upset at the Church's stance on same-sex marriage and other LGBT issues, women who felt they weren't welcome in the Church, or the children of divorced parents who felt they were ostracized in their parishes. Others were surely just being hateful. But either way, unless I wanted to take the risk of a pleasant conversation going sour, I became more vague about the nature of my work. This put to rest any possible visceral reactions to Catholicism and allowed me to get to know people and form friendships. But all that has seemed to change under Pope Francis.

Today, when I tell people I cover the Church, they still have something to say, but it's usually something about Francis. Comments range from curiosity to fascination to outright fawning, but there's hardly ever a negative reaction. This makes conversation much more pleasant. Personally, as a young Catholic who's watched most of my friends and relatives drift away from their faith, I see hope for the future in Francis. Sure, he can't single-handedly change challenging demographic trends overnight. But Francis's papacy, and his Tweeting, give me hope that he might motivate my generation of believers not to give up on the Church just yet. The reason is simple: Jesus. This pope knows the world needs the teachings of Jesus, and he's showing us firsthand how that looks. He invites us to be stakeholders in his papacy via Twitter, connecting directly with him and in the process becoming responsible for the solution. We can't be passive bystanders.

Some of the pope's critics lament his off-the-cuff style, believing erroneously that this is a man without a plan. But a close examination of the pope's Tweets proves otherwise (which is what the rest of this book will demonstrate). Looking at the pope's more than six hundred Tweets, it is easy to identify several core themes and causes the pope seeks to highlight, and Twitter has become perhaps his most successful preaching platform.

Though Francis is adamant and explicit that the Church must adapt and reflect more closely the life of its founder, Jesus, there are still those who seek to undermine his message. Think of how often Francis has said something extraordinary in an interview, only to have bastions of the old guard say, "No, he didn't mean that. Let me explain what he *really* meant," and go on to spin the pope's words to fit their own agendas. Sometimes these voices are the loudest, and the pope's message can be drowned out. But there's another way: connecting with the pope directly on Twitter. There lies a direct channel between Francis and millions of believers around the world. The messages are concise and direct, not susceptible to the dismissive tone of those seeking to prop up the old ways. Of course, many of those 140-character messages are simply the tip of the iceberg. *The Tweetable Pope* puts them in context, and gives readers the ability to understand fully what the pope has in mind: his passions, priorities, and plans.

But it's not just about power. The pope isn't a celebrity seeking to enhance his brand. Through Twitter, Francis seeks to offer encouragement, teach the faithful, and, sometimes, even challenge them to change their lives. That's how he'll change the Church. Twitter gives a hint of this man's magnetic personality, something I was fortunate enough to witness firsthand during the 2014 Synod on the Family in Rome.

One morning during the synod, I was part of the press pool that was given access to the Synod Hall. This is where cardinals and bishops were gathered to discuss hot-button issues like divorce, homosexuality, and how to keep families strong in an increasingly secular society. I entered the Synod Hall, and two things struck me immediately. First, this wasn't the

Sistine Chapel, with incense and sacred chants filling the air. It was more like a college lecture hall, with drop-down projector screens, PowerPoint slides, and mundane computer monitors. Just like the pope's presence on Twitter, the modern technology at first seemed to jar with this ancient Church. The pope and his aides sat on the dais, facing the synod participants in their stadium-style seats. Many wore headphones to hear translations. Morning prayers were projected on the screens. Even with all this technology, the synod fathers were told that they were not allowed to Tweet during the synod itself. Ironic given that many cardinals and bishops had joined Twitter to follow the pope's example. And even just a couple of years into Tweeting, it was difficult for some of them to be away from their virtual flocks.

Journalists are invited in for two reasons: to get a sense of the surroundings and to get some face time with cardinals and bishops. When I entered, those men who would make decisions affecting millions of Catholics around the world were milling around. Some were engaged in what seemed to be serious conversation. Others shared a laugh before the day began. A few sipped their Americanos to amp up for the long day ahead. The calm, relaxed environment was not what I had anticipated.

Suddenly, a man in a white zucchetto and matching cassock entered from a door down below. Pope Francis! But there was no fanfare, and the cardinals and bishops kept talking and laughing. I wondered, would the cardinals be embarrassed, some with their backs toward the Holy Father? Would they immediately proceed to their seats, and wait for the Vicar of Christ to begin the day in prayer? Nope. They kept on chatting. Sipping coffee. Telling jokes. Francis, from my vantage point, joined in, with a big smile on his face. He seemed to be relaxed, either unaware or unconcerned of the media circus that had developed over the previous days. (Things outside the Synod Hall had gotten so crazy that a major news personality on one of America's largest networks was featured in a special report, "Exclusive: Watch Pope Francis wave to our reporter as he enters the Synod!")

This laid-back atmosphere, I would later be told, was something new, encouraged by Francis so that ideas could be exchanged freely. From the top down, the tone had changed. Things had become so relaxed, one cardinal told me, that during the coffee breaks around 10:30 each morning, bishops would run up to the pope, hoping either to press their case further or simply to share an insight from the first two hours of work. Because the pope doesn't like people serving him, he made his way to the coffee bar himself. But because the synod fathers felt so comfortable approaching him, a throng of admirers often blocked his path. This meant on several mornings, he wasn't able to get a cup of coffee at all, being hurried back to his seat as the break ended.

This atmosphere meant that some synod fathers would feel free to put forward ideas once verboten in the Church, which would add to the drama over the coming days. To see the pope in person, to be about thirty feet from him, I could feel in my gut that something had changed. That environment in the Synod Hall is one that Francis wants for the whole Church, and one he advocates for on Twitter. He can tell his cardinals and bishops face-to-face that they should feel comfortable saying what's on their minds. For Catholics in the pews, Francis uses Twitter to do the same thing.

As my time in Rome was winding down, I found myself at dinner with a priest who works in the Vatican. After finishing a delicious Roman meal, along with a couple of glasses of wine that, in Rome, cost less than a can of Diet Coke, we departed the restaurant. Once we realized we were going the same way, he decided we should cut through Saint Peter's Square. It was a perfectly clear, crisp October evening, with Bernini's illuminated columns and Michelangelo's majestic dome providing a rather dramatic backdrop to our stroll. He directed me to a place in the middle of the square that provides unparalleled views of this sacred space. I was moved by my surroundings, reflecting on the week I had just experienced. "Michael," the priest said to me, "take a look around." He was pointing to the majesty of it all. Here it comes, I thought. A bit of inside wisdom, maybe something the pope had said in private that I could ruminate on during my long flight home. "Michael, nowhere else on earth can you cram more dysfunction into one square mile than right here. Welcome to the Vatican!"

Not exactly what I had in mind, but the joke made me laugh and it's stuck with me. It captures what "the Church" is to so many: at once inspiring and lofty, but simultaneously human and faulty. This is the Church that Pope Francis wants to reform, make more relevant to people, and put in dialogue with the modern world. How does any person, even with the title "pope," hope to change an institution with one billion members spread all over the globe? Twitter is part of his answer and strategy. It is a tool, a modern medium for an ancient Church. The charismatic Francis may have mastered Twitter, but the story begins with his quiet and decidedly more introverted predecessor.

Pope Benedict XVI Makes History—Twice

Before Pope Francis took the world—and Twitter—by storm, another pope had to make history. A couple of weeks before Francis greeted the millions tuned in with a gentle "good evening" from a balcony overlooking Saint Peter's Square, Pope Benedict XVI had been whisked away in a helicopter to the pope's summer residence fifteen miles southeast of Rome, Castel Gandolfo. Of course, this was March, not August when popes usually vacation, and Benedict wouldn't be returning to the

Vatican, at least not as pope. Benedict had become the first pope in centuries to resign from office.

Despite his best efforts at reform, and despite his sharp theological mind, Benedict's papacy had been overrun by scandal. After betrayal at the hands of his personal butler, who leaked sensitive documents to the press in order to embarrass key members of the Roman Curia, the German pontiff said he was no longer up to the job. Benedict's decision to resign, to give up the trappings of office and to break with centuries of Catholic tradition, will undoubtedly be the hallmark of his legacy, a move praised by his fans and critics alike. But this wasn't the only history the German-born pontiff had made as pope.

Two months before he vacated the Chair of Peter, flanked by colorful Swiss Guards, he did something millions of people do every day without much thought. He tapped out a few characters on a black iPad and hit send. But this wasn't just anybody; it was the pope, the Vicar of Christ on Earth. And with just a few clicks, on December 12, 2012, he thrust one of the oldest institutions on earth into the heart of the digital age.

 Benedict XVI @Pontifex • 12 December 2012
Dear friends, I am pleased to get
in touch with you through Twitter.
Thank you for your generous response.
I bless all of you from my heart.

It was a somewhat strange sight, a frail, white-haired eighty-five-year-old German trying out new technology. Known for writing moving, if somewhat dense, encyclicals and theological books, he nonetheless embraced the 140-character limit in order to help spread the faith. In the few weeks between the arrival of @Pontifex—"bridge builder" in Latin—and the end of his papacy, Benedict sent 39 Tweets. In the process, he amassed more than 3 million followers on his 8 language accounts, including Arabic.

Benedict's Tweets aren't particularly memorable, given that the Vatican was still figuring out how best to use the social media platform. But that he used the platform at all remains revolutionary. He embraced a new method of communication, and in the process he raised the bar for what's expected of Church leaders. People no longer want whitewashed messages delivered through prepared statements. They want to hear directly from celebrities, politicians, activists, and now popes. Benedict obliged. But on February 28, 2013, Benedict sent his final message:

 Benedict XVI @Pontifex • 28 February 2013

Thank you for your love and support. May you always experience the joy that comes from putting Christ at the centre of your lives.

The day after this Tweet, the world's 1.2 billion Catholics were without a shepherd in Rome. The Church had entered the *sede vacante,* or the time of "the seat being vacant." This centuries-old custom took on a modern flair, as well. The descriptor for the @Pontifex account was changed to "Sede Vacante" and all of Pope Benedict's Tweets were deleted. (Like centuries of ancient documents, his thirty-nine Tweets were moved to the Vatican archives, this time stored on servers, not shelves.) His eventual successor would be handed not only the keys to the Kingdom of Heaven, but, perhaps more importantly in this digital age, the password to the papal Twitter account—and its millions of followers.

The World Waits

Television cameras descended on Rome immediately after Benedict departed to live his new monastic life. They were mounted on rooftops surrounding the Vatican, trained carefully on Saint Peter's for any hint on the future of the Church. Who would the 115 cardinals choose to lead the Church following a turbulent decade? Was campaigning going on behind the scenes, even if Church law forbids such politicking? Would the Italians take control after decades of rule from first a Pole and then a German?

When the cardinals finally sealed themselves into the Sistine Chapel on March 12, 2013, the journalists gathered in Rome had already exhausted their cache of "color" stories. Usually there's a papal funeral in the two weeks leading up to a papal election, giving Catholics around the world something to watch. This time, there was no such event, but people were still hungry for news. Something had to fill the void, and what did gave a hint into the place that Twitter would have during the next papacy.

Elected in 2005, Benedict was the first pope to take charge during the Internet age. At that time, the web still functioned as a place where users primarily consumed information. But by 2013, the democratization of news gathering and sharing on social networks like Twitter had reached entirely new levels. Catholics, and curious Church watchers, could participate in this conclave in wholly new ways, not least of which would be Twitter. For many, the "SMS of the web" was both a primary news source and a place for conversation about that news. The papal election would be no different.

When things go as planned, there is no actual news to report when cardinals are sequestered in the Sistine Chapel. They are barred by sacred oath from speaking about what happens inside Michelangelo's masterpiece. They communicate with the world not by electronic messages, but with straw, burned with the aid of chemicals, colored either black, to signify no pope has been elected, or white, announcing that a new pope has been chosen.

For two days, the world waited, but there wasn't

much going on. But that didn't stop Catholic Tweeps—slang for Twitter friends or followers—from participating in the excitement. That eagerness to feel like we were part of the action went off the rails when a fairly unremarkable bird suddenly took center stage on the second day of the election.

Countless webcams and news crews were streaming live shots of the chimney above the Sistine Chapel, even though there was no sign of action inside. A common seagull suddenly flew into the frame, circled a few times, and then took a break, right there, on the most watched chimney in the world. Hey, there wasn't a new pope, but this bird was something.

Within minutes, #Seagull became a worldwide trending topic—one of the most popular topics of digital conversation on Twitter. Multiple parody accounts were launched. One, @SistineSeagull, attracted more than 8,000 followers; another, @ConclaveChimney, attracted 10,000. The average Twitter user has just over 60 followers. (This famously serene seagull would provide something of an unfortunate contrast a few months later, when two children standing next to Pope Francis would release a pair of peace doves into the air, only to see them mauled, one by a crow and the other, ironically, by a seagull. No word if the perpetrator was the Sistine Seagull, perhaps envious of the doves' new fame.)

The popularity of the Sistine Seagull captured the desire of Catholics to be part of the historic event, to be in community, even if it's through an online platform. It also showed how little actual news there is during a conclave. But it wouldn't be long before there was actual news to report. The following evening, just after seven o'clock local time on March 13, crowds gathered in Saint Peter's Square. Those following along at home on Twitter and other social media sites broke into applause at the site of white smoke. The Church had a pope.

The *sede vacante* was over, both in reality and on Twitter. About thirty minutes following his election, @Pontifex returned. The first Tweet of the Francis era had been sent.

 Pope Francis @Pontifex • 13 March 2013
HABEMUS PAPAM FRANCISCUM

As church bells throughout Rome rang to herald the news, the @Pontifex account proclaimed "HABEMUS PAPAM FRANCISCUM" ("We have a pope! Francis!"), digitally announcing the traditional first words announced from the balcony overlooking Saint Peter's. It didn't take long for more than 70,000 people to join in the celebrations by re-Tweeting to their followers.

A new papacy was afoot, and though the world didn't yet know it, so was a new way of connecting everyday Catholics to their spiritual leader. The Tweetable Pope was powering up.

The Tweets That Started It All

Just four days after election, Pope Francis was still an unknown entity to most people around the world. Of course, he had charmed the millions gathered with him in person and those watching online when he stepped out onto the balcony overlooking Saint Peter's, with his simple, down-to-earth speech and mannerisms. He wished the gathered pilgrims a good evening and asked them for their blessing before he bestowed the traditional first papal blessing. As the evening came to a close, Francis, still a blank slate, told people to get home safely, like a close friend saying good night.

Then, he delivered a special message to the followers he'd inherited from his predecessor.

 Pope Francis @Pontifex • 17 March 2013

Dear friends, I thank you from my heart and I ask you to continue to pray for me. Pope Francis.

Nothing particularly revelatory, but a sign he'd keep the papal Twitter account going.

In the coming days, Pope Francis published Tweets that offered real insight into both his priorities for the Church and his vision of the papacy. These two short, seemingly inconsequential messages are quite remarkable, knowing what we know now. His first message highlighted concern for creation.

Pope Francis @Pontifex • 19 March 2013

Let us keep a place for Christ in our lives, let us care for one another and let us be loving custodians of creation.

Two years later, he would release an encyclical about the duty Catholics have in caring for creation. It's the first papal document devoted entirely to the topic. Many had hoped that this pope's chosen name—Francis, after the thirteenth-century Italian saint concerned with nature and the poor—might give insight into his priorities. This Tweet affirmed those hopes. It was a prelude for the pope who would say, "Enough is enough," calling on Catholics to act and to care for creation that has suffered at the hands of greed for too long.

 Pope Francis @Pontifex • 19 March 2013

True power is service. The Pope must serve all people, especially the poor, the weak, the vulnerable.

Francis's third Tweet, above, explains his view of the papacy. His main concern is not making sure Rome's power is preserved and respected, but that it is characterized by "service." Francis was elected by his peers to clean up the mess that had plagued Pope Benedict in his final years as pope: careerist, self-aggrandizing clerics driven by greed and willing to use blackmail to further their insatiable thirst for power. No, Pope Francis was saying, this is not how pastors act. Rather, they are to be with their people, accompanying them through life's ups and downs. He would go on to use his famous image of the Church as a field hospital, saying pastors must smell of sheep. Remarkably, hints of the pope's priorities were right there on Twitter from the first week of his papacy.

Inside the Vatican's Twitter Command Center

Spoiler alert: Pope Francis doesn't hit send on his own Tweets. In fact, the only time a pope has published a Tweet was the first time, when Pope Benedict nudged the Vatican into the digital world. But Francis comes up with the ideas for his Tweets. The messages are printed in Italian or Spanish, the pope's two primary languages, and brought to the pope. Once he signs off, they're taken back to the Vatican Secretary of State's office. This is significant.

The Vatican has a huge, lumbering communications program, with a radio station, newspaper, multiple websites, apps, and even a YouTube channel. But Twitter's power to communicate to the world is clear to the Holy See, and they housed it in the Vatican's main diplomatic branch. From there, the Tweets are published in Italian, and then translated into eight other languages: English, Spanish, German, Polish, Portuguese, French, Arabic, and Latin.

This focus on Twitter as diplomacy has worked. A group that tracks the influence of global leaders on Twitter has named Pope Francis the most influential Tweeting global leader three years in a row. President Barack Obama, the world's most followed political leader, may have three times as many followers as Francis, but the pope's followers are more invested in his Tweets. They re-Tweet the pope at far higher levels than any other leader. The second most influential leader, Saudi Arabia's King Salman, has an engagement rate less than half of the pope's. With nearly 10,000 re-Tweets per message, one of the pope's 140-character messages reaches many times more than the nearly 30 million followers who receive it directly.

Twitter is for many people their primary method of gathering news, taking part in an online community, and now, connecting with the pope. During the pope's January 2015 visit to the Philippines, for example, more than 3.3 million Tweets were posted about Pope Francis in that country in just seven days. When the pope touched down in Manila, Filipinos sent 4,000 papal-related Tweets each second, breaking new social media records there. In preparation for his September 2015 visit to the United States, wireless giants AT&T and Verizon provided portable cell towers so pilgrims could Tweet their experiences in real time.

Even though Francis isn't personally counting characters, he's fully invested in the power behind social media to impact lives. He wants his Tweets to engage his followers: encouraging them, giving them a lift, and even challenging them once in a while. Though Francis hasn't responded to any of his followers personally, responses help him keep track of what his flock considers important, what's on their minds. In the United States and the United Kingdom, lots of people use Twitter to express their frustration about the clergy sex abuse crisis or the Church's views on sexuality. But in Italy and Spain, Tweets roll in about excesses in the Church. Whether or not Francis will ever use Twitter to engage some of his followers directly remains to be seen, but he's open to the idea. For a pope who telephones Catholics who've written him letters, the notion of replying to a Tweet or two doesn't seem that unlikely.

Given the incredible success of Twitter, a bright spot in the Vatican's sprawling communications program, it's shocking that no single person is tasked with managing the pope's Twitter account. Instead, a small team of five people devote some of their time to helping get the pope's message out. They know which messages the pope wants out there, which causes are most dear to his heart. Sometimes, Francis lends his name to an ongoing Twitter campaign, like he did with #BringBackOurGirls, the online effort to raise awareness about Boko Haram's notorious kidnappings of Nigerian schoolgirls. Other times, Francis uses his online clout to create entirely new movements, like he did with #PrayForPeace, his campaign to stop Western-led military campaigns in war-torn Syria. Though he's able to help the world focus its attention on suffering Iraqis or victims of devastating typhoons, the pope's fun side comes out on Twitter once in a while, too. An avid soccer fan, Francis was caught up in the excitement surrounding the World Cup, congratulating players and fans via Twitter. He's Tweeted at badly behaved bishops, urging them to stop gossiping, and he's entered the fiercest debates, including ones about economic inequality.

Francis upped his Twitter game in June 2015 to coincide with the release of *Laudato Si'*, or Praise Be to You, the first papal encyclical devoted to the environment. I was in Rome covering the release of the document when I was given a heads-up that there would be some Twitter news to accompany the unveiling. Moments later, as the press conference was concluding, a Vatican spokesperson announced that Francis would unleash a "Twitterbomb" later in the day. For twenty-four hours straight, Francis would Tweet short excerpts from his nearly two-hundred-page encyclical, definitely a papal first. We'll go further into this in chapter 7.

The most powerful Tweets, however, are those aimed at Francis's spiritual revolution. This pope was elected to clean up the Church. His allies aren't bureaucrats in Rome, who sank his predecessor's efforts. They're the people of God, the vast majority of ordinary Catholics like the ones Francis ministered to and lived alongside in Buenos Aires. Twitter gives Francis direct access to these folks and he's not wasting a single character. He wants the Church to focus on its founder, Jesus. That's why he and his Tweets highlight mercy, the poor, and service. The three most frequently used unique words in all the pope's more than six hundred Tweets, in fact, are "God," "love," and "Jesus." But even the frequency of common words is telling. Topping the list are "us," "we," and "our." The pope's Tweets are all aimed at making ours a truly welcoming Church, based on the love of God and teachings of Jesus. Francis will change the Church by pushing his followers toward spiritual renewal.

Following the Tweetable Pope

Some say that Catholics are still trying to understand the pope's priorities and his vision for the future of the papacy. But really, it was all laid out right there, just five days after his election, 140 characters at a time. By looking at these Tweets, and the more than 600 he's sent since then, we get a bit closer to what this Tweetable pope has in mind for the Church and its billion members.

Even a quick glance at the pope's Tweets gives his followers a sense of his passions, priorities, and plans for the Church. For *The Tweetable Pope,* however, I dug deeper than most of the pope's followers have time for. I categorized each Tweet based on several themes that jumped out at me. Some of them became obvious quite quickly, based solely on keywords. For example, Francis has Tweeted about Jesus and God close to two hundred times, totaling nearly one-third of his Tweets. This makes sense given his role as pope. Prayer is another example, with more than fifty Tweets explicitly about prayer—how to do it and why it's important—and dozens more asking for prayers for the passions close to the pope's heart.

Other themes require a bit more analysis. Take life issues for example. In the United States, describing oneself as pro-life is often shorthand for opposition to abortion. With this understanding in mind, explicit Tweets about the Church's traditional pro-life cause are rare; there are only a few. But by understanding that Francis wants those concerned with life to think about more than just abortion—such as the elderly, the disabled, and the lonely—we find that the pope actually Tweets about life issues more often than might appear at first glance.

Of course there are plenty of Tweets about Jesus and prayer. Talking about those things is a pope's job. But there are the other themes that are evident only to those who scrutinize this pope on a daily basis, what a journalist like yours truly might have the time to do. And these often give the most accurate reflection of what's on this pope's mind. Gossip is a good example. Francis has only Tweeted explicitly about the scourge of gossip a couple of times. But because I read many of his homilies and follow events in the Church, well, religiously, I know that stopping gossip is a major concern for Francis. In *The Tweetable Pope,* I take these two Tweets and put them into a wider context, offering further insight and analysis into the Francis Revolution.

These kinds of seemingly rare Tweets are often the most interesting. But they're also the easiest to overlook, with topics such as sports, work, inequality, and the devil taking up a relatively small percentage of real estate on the pope's Twitter feed but offering huge clues into his papacy. "Easter eggs" is Internet speak for hidden treats on the web for those in the know, clues for those who understand what to look for. That's what these Tweets are, and *The Tweetable Pope* invites readers to join the club, to know what to look for and why it's important. The pope's "Easter eggs" offer many clues into where he intends to lead the Church as well as how Christians should live their lives to emulate Jesus more closely.

This pope says what's on his mind in ways that ordinary, salt-of-the-earth believers can understand. He repeatedly ditches prepared texts so that he can engage in conversation with his audience. His off-the-cuff homilies speak to the real needs of Catholics and non-Catholics alike. And his impromptu press conferences aboard the papal plane are where the real news happens. But you don't need to examine the pope's every speech and homily or be a member of the Vatican press corps to understand and be inspired by this papacy. Rather, access to a free Twitter account along with *The Tweetable Pope* will give anyone interested in this remarkable papacy the ability to track trends and put short thoughts into their proper context.

And here's that context. For all the hype around Pope Francis—and he undoubtedly deserves much of it given the way he's reinvigorated the faith lives of so many—it's not about him. He doesn't use Twitter to burnish his self-image or sell a product. He Tweets to preach ancient truths in a uniquely modern way. He'd undoubtedly be the first to agree with these 58 characters: If you love Pope Francis, wait until you hear about Jesus.

2

Prayer

IF YOU TAKE JUST THREE THINGS AWAY FROM *THE TWEETABLE Pope*, make it these: Jesus, God, and prayer. Those are Pope Francis's three priorities on Twitter. As of this writing, he's mentioned Jesus (or Christ, or Jesus Christ) 132 times, God 123 times, and prayer 99 times. As I wrote in chapter 1, this is hardly surprising given the pope's job description. But what's so fascinating is how prayer is such an integral part of all the pope's work. From pressuring the United States not to bomb Syria, to condemning terrorists in Africa, to simple notes of encouragement to his virtual flock, prayer seems to be invoked almost every time. Francis asks for prayers for a range of things, as we see in his Tweets.

Pope Francis @Pontifex • 8 January 2015

#PrayersForParis

Pope Francis @Pontifex • 10 June 2014

Let us pray for all victims of sexual violence in conflict, and those working to end this crime. #TimeToAct

Pope Francis @Pontifex • 22 May 2015

Lord, send forth your Holy Spirit to bring consolation and strength to persecuted Christians. #free2pray

Pope Francis @Pontifex • 9 September 2013

Humanity needs to see these gestures of peace and to hear words of hope and peace! #prayforpeace

Pope Francis @Pontifex • 12 May 2013

Let us pray for the many Christians in the world who still suffer persecution and violence. May God grant them the courage of fidelity.

Francis knows he talks about prayer quite a bit. In a general audience in May 2014, he acknowledged as much, joking, "We always return to the same theme: prayer! Yet prayer is so important." Undeterred by what others think, he devoted the next several minutes giving some tips on fitting prayer into our hectic and chaotic lives. "Never forget prayer. Never! No one, no one realizes when we pray on the bus, on the road: we pray in the silence of our heart. Let us take advantage of these moments to pray." The pope frequently asks for prayers for his diplomatic missions and for tragedies around the world, as you see above, but he also uses Twitter to ask us to pray more in our own lives in order to connect with God. There's no agenda in these Tweets, other than encouraging his followers to slow down and reach out to God.

 Pope Francis @Pontifex • 24 May 2013

Miracles happen. But prayer is needed! Prayer that is courageous, struggling and persevering, not prayer that is a mere formality.

 Pope Francis @Pontifex • 13 March 2014

Please pray for me.

Pope Francis @Pontifex • 4 October 2014

As Jesus told Martha in the Gospel, one thing is necessary: prayer. #praywithus

Even if we agree that prayer is important, how is Francis getting anything done if he's praying or soliciting prayers on Twitter so often? Well, Francis rejects the premise of that question. We've become accustomed to separating our prayer from the rest of life; one part is sacred, the other profane. That's not the case. Drawing on his Jesuit tradition, Francis wants us to view the entirety of our lives through a lens of prayer. All that we do should be prayer in some sense, and Francis is teaching us on Twitter how to live more integrated lives.

 Pope Francis @Pontifex • 17 October 2013

Our prayer cannot be reduced to an hour on Sundays. It is important to have a daily relationship with the Lord.

 Pope Francis @Pontifex • 3 May 2013

It would be a good idea, during May, for families to say the Rosary together. Prayer strengthens family life.

Pope Francis @Pontifex • 17 June 2013
Are you angry with someone? Pray for that person. That is what Christian love is.

Prayer, as we can see, plays a big part in Francis's life, though that doesn't mean he's distracted from other things, like reforming a global institution. In fact, prayer is one of the ways he's able to balance so much. Much of the answer to that seeming paradox—having so much time for prayer while staying so busy—lies in his Jesuit background and his emphasis on Ignatian spirituality.

Saint Ignatius of Loyola was a sixteenth-century Spanish soldier who suffered a serious injury in battle. During his convalescence he experienced a powerful conversion while reading about the lives of the saints. Once healed, he founded what would become the Jesuit order, or the Society of Jesus, in 1540. Aside from launching a religious community that would go on to become "the Church's marines," spreading Catholicism around the globe and establishing some of the world's great universities, Ignatius also gifted to the Church one of its great spiritual treasures, aptly named the Spiritual Exercises.

At its most basic, the Exercises are a rubric for a four-week retreat in which participants imagine themselves being with Jesus, helping to open themselves up to where God is at work in their lives today. Part of the Exercises involves the application of the senses, mentally placing ourselves alongside Jesus in order to make his life more relevant to ours. Even today, nearly five hundred years after the order was launched, all Jesuits, including Francis, still practice the Exercises at least twice in their lives. In fact, the Exercises have been adapted in such a way that one could incorporate them into daily life, spanning a nine-month period. The idea that prayer is something to add into one's life, instead of something that is fully integrated, is nonsense.

But beyond this retreat, which is also offered in shorter durations for priests, religious, and laypeople, the Exercises have produced a certain incarnational spirituality that "finds God in all things" and encourages believers to be "contemplatives in action." Prayer should not be seen as an escape from real life but as a resource, guide, and comfort for diving more deeply into real life. These two hallmarks of Ignatian spirituality—*contemplation* and *action*—seem to drive everything Francis does as pope, including his exhortations to prayer. (For a much more thorough explanation of Jesuit life and Ignatian spirituality, I recommend *The Jesuit Guide to (Almost) Everything* by my friend and Jesuit priest Rev. James Martin, SJ.)

Jesuits don't sit around praying all day. They get out in the world, interacting with God's people and doing God's work. Though a religious order, Jesuits aren't monks. Don't get me wrong, I love monks. I have many Benedictine monk friends, some from my undergraduate days at Saint Anselm College and some newer pals who help me translate Italian when I'm over in Rome. I once asked one of these friends, what's the point of monks? He thought for a moment and said, "To pray for the world." I like it.

But Francis isn't a monk. He's a Jesuit, and his job is to pray and act, or in Ignatius's own words, to be a "contemplative in action." As busy as we all are, we sometimes push prayer to a few minutes before we fall asleep, if we're lucky. But Francis wants us to consider another way. Maybe we can find God during all the craziness, perhaps with the help of technology we hold in the palms of our hands. That's the beauty of Twitter.

 Pope Francis @Pontifex • 28 June 2014

To be friends with God means to pray with simplicity, like children talking to their parents.

 Pope Francis @Pontifex • 20 May 2014

Come, Holy Spirit! Help us to overcome our selfishness.

Many people complain that Twitter is shortening our attention spans, distracting us from our work, and making us obsess about the most trivial matters. But when Pope Francis Tweets about prayer, as he so often does, we can put his Tweets to work to combat some of the negative side effects of social media. If you follow Francis, or follow folks who follow and re-Tweet Francis, it's inevitable that you'll eventually see a Tweet about prayer pop up on your timeline. Rather than another distraction, view it as an invitation to close your eyes, even for ten seconds, and just breathe. Don't ask for anything, don't recite a Hail Mary or Our Father, and don't worry if you're praying "correctly." Just sit there, in silence, and breathe. This, believe it or not, is prayer, and it might just be the kind of prayer Francis wants us to pray most.

When asked by Rev. Antonio Spadaro, SJ, the editor of *La Civiltà Cattolica*, what traits of Ignatian spirituality would help the first Jesuit pope do his job, Francis replied with one word: "discernment." Discernment, more or less, means listening to God's will before one acts. When done well, discernment "means being able to do the little things of every day with a big heart open to God," Francis said.

Children are taught to memorize prayers, and many people stop learning how to pray during childhood. So for many people, prayer remains simply reciting a series of memorized words and phrases. It runs the risk of losing meaning if we're not careful. Francis wants us to quiet our minds for a moment or two and be still, "looking at the signs, listening to the things that happen."

The Tweetable pope put it another, perhaps more memorable, way during a morning homily in October 2013. "The Lord tells us," he said, "'the first task in life is this: prayer.' But not the prayer of words, like a parrot; but the prayer [of the] heart: gazing on the Lord, hearing the Lord, asking the Lord." Don't pray like a parrot, simply mimicking the words you've been taught. (*Crux,* the *Boston Globe*'s website I write for, runs a series called TGIF, publishing humorous Catholic-related items from around the web each Friday. One of the most popular items remains a parrot that was trained to sing the Hail Mary. Fun, yes, but Francis wants more from his flock than this.)

Instead, imagine yourself with Jesus, and listen to what he has to say to you. That's the pope's message for us: be quiet and listen. If we don't, he warns, we run the risk of "closing the door to the Lord, so that he can do nothing." When we pray, the pope says, we open the door to God, who "knows to arrange things, to reorganize things. This is what praying is: opening the door to the Lord, so that he can do something" in our lives.

One of the pope's closest advisers, Boston's Cardinal Seán O'Malley, said in a speech at a Jesuit university in Baltimore in March 2014 that the key to understanding Francis's papacy is becoming familiar with the pope's Jesuit heritage. O'Malley, a Franciscan, recalled that Ignatius, after finishing his study of the saints, reportedly said he wanted to live a life like that of Saint Francis, the thirteenth-century Italian who eschewed familial wealth in order to serve the poor and rebuild the Church. Ignatius would go on to become a saint in his own right. Today, the Church is blessed with a leader who seems to exude the traits of both men. "Well, we have a pope who has embraced the vocation of being a follower of Ignatius, who wanted to be a saint like Saint Francis," O'Malley said.

O'Malley credits the pope's daily examen, another prayer inspired by Ignatius. The examen is an attempt to reflect on one's daily activities to discern where God is present. As O'Malley put it, the examen "was Ignatius's plan to keep the Jesuits recollected in God-focused lives despite their active lifestyle." Francis wants us to find God in all things, and sometimes this takes a little extra time. The examen can be intense, with journaling, silent reflection, and a deep commitment to explore each and every action of each and every day, searching for moments of grace. But it doesn't have to be too onerous, and Francis is using Twitter to invite us to make mini-examens part of our daily routines. Next time a papal prayer request pops up in under 140 characters, perhaps you can step back and consider where God is present, or distant, in your life.

In addition to Jesuit spirituality, Francis has a particular devotion to Mary, as evidenced by his many Tweets about her. The pope has a special love for Jesus's mother, and he invites his followers to join him in this uniquely Catholic spirituality.

Pope Francis @Pontifex • 2 September 2014

The Christian who does not feel that the Virgin Mary is his or her mother is an orphan.

Pope Francis @Pontifex • 31 May 2014

In the difficult moments of life, Christians can turn to the Mother of God and find protection and care.

Pope Francis @Pontifex • 15 August 2014

Mary, Queen of Heaven, help us to transform the world according to God's plan.

For Francis, prayer isn't something separate from the hustle and bustle of everyday living, a luxury reserved for chanting monks. (Sorry again, Benedictines!) Rather, life itself is one great big prayer, unfolding in our interactions with others and those moments when we find ourselves alone. We just need to slow down, even for a few seconds now and then, to find God, and listen to what God's saying. That might mean closing Twitter and stepping away from the iPad for a minute or two, but the reminder to do this might very well show up in a short message from @Pontifex sometime soon.

3

Mercy

NEARLY 10 PERCENT OF THE POPE'S TWEETS INCLUDE THE word "mercy." This is no accident. Part of the pope's ambitious renewal effort is to make the Church more merciful. Rather than a place where sinners feel judged, Francis envisions a Church where people turn for comfort. His point is that we are all sinners, even our beloved popes, and the Church must respond to this reality with mercy, not condemnation.

"I am a sinner," the pope said when asked who he is by the Jesuit journal *La Civiltà Cattolica*—a line he's repeated many times since. Embracing a man whose face is covered in boils, washing the feet of a young Muslim woman, praying with the disabled: the most iconic images of this papacy are rooted in mercy. What Francis has modeled conveys a simple truth—mainly that Jesus's ministry was rooted in mercy, and our interactions with our families, friends, neighbors, and fellow Christians should be as well—from Francis himself as the Bishop of Rome to his cardinals, bishops, and priests, all the way to religious and laypeople who comprise the majority of the Catholic Church. The goal is a more merciful world, ushered in by a more merciful Church.

Pope Francis @Pontifex • 23 March 2015

May every Church and Christian community be a place of mercy amid so much indifference.

Pope Francis @Pontifex • 28 October 2014

May we help people to discover the joy of the Christian message: a message of love and mercy.

Four days after his election, Francis preached Mass in the chapel at his residence, Casa Santa Marta. He said, quite simply, mercy is the Lord's most powerful gift. Even the most casual observer of the Francis papacy must realize that this sentiment drives so much of what the pope does.

Pope Francis @Pontifex • 26 September 2013

God's forgiveness is stronger than any sin.

Pope Francis @Pontifex • 19 May 2015

God is always waiting for us, he always understands us, he always forgives us.

As the Jesuit priest and author James Martin noted in *The Washington Post,* there were many possible story lines following Francis's historic visit to Rio for the 2013 World Youth Day: record crowds, security mishaps, and the best indication to date that Francis was a global superstar. But the one that took the media by storm was the pope's off-the-cuff remarks about mercy, spoken from the papal plane en route back to Rome. Francis was asked about gay priests, but he zoomed out a bit to talk about gay people generally. "If a gay person is searching for God, who am I to judge?" he replied. (I'm sure I wasn't alone when I thought, *You're the pope, that's who!)* The second part of that line was just as extraordinary. "They should not be marginalized," he said. Something new was in the air, and it wasn't the Alitalia aircraft.

When Pope Francis was Archbishop of Buenos Aires, the Argentine government was pushing a same-sex marriage law. The Catholic bishops there were vehemently opposed to it and they planned to campaign against the measure. Behind the scenes, however, Cardinal Jorge Bergoglio, as Francis was then known, floated a compromise. Perhaps the bishops could support civil unions for same-sex couples and avoid a nasty fight over marriage. Cynics say it was a ploy to limit the rights of gay couples, to keep marriage exclusively for heterosexuals. Given that Francis has proven himself a shrewd tactician and skilled political operative, it's more likely that Francis understood the need for mercy.

The pope shares the Church's belief that marriage is a union between one man and one woman, but he also recognizes that life's a little messier than that neat rubric suggests. Before he was "the pope of mercy," Francis was a pastor. Though he never indicated a desire to change Church teaching about marriage, he did show a preference for mercy.

Life is tough, a reality Francis knows firsthand from his time spent with the poor in the outskirts of Buenos Aires. He's mentioned with sadness on more than one occasion the single moms he met who couldn't find a priest willing to baptize their children. He's lamented that the poor didn't feel welcome in parishes, and as a result that they were deprived of spiritual edification. But you don't have to live in a slum to understand this reality. Individuals from all walks of life experience loneliness, give in to temptation, or end up living in arrangements that aren't always in accord with the demands of Catholic teaching. Oftentimes, people in situations like these fear that instead of mercy, the Church offers only judgment. Francis wants this to change, but it won't be easy. It'll take more than a few key Curial changes and appointing the right kinds of bishops. Instead, all Catholics, including the 21 million or so who follow him on Twitter, must transform our hearts. It's on Twitter that Francis communicates directly with Catholics, exhorting them both to accept God's mercy in their lives, and to pay it forward to others. If in the past some Catholics saw their roles as guardians of mercy, Francis reminds his followers that mercy is a gift for all, especially those who need it most.

Francis described his vision for a Church of mercy quite beautifully in September 2013, when calling for believers "to heal wounds and to warm the hearts of the faithful." He stressed that such mercy "needs nearness, proximity." The Church, he said, should be "a field hospital after battle. It is useless to ask a seriously injured person if he has high cholesterol and about the level of his blood sugars! You have to heal his wounds." When a patient comes into an emergency room, doctors don't ask why he was shot, whether he did something to prompt the attack. They show mercy, they heal. A merciful Church is the kind of Church Francis envisions.

 Pope Francis @Pontifex • 13 May 2014

Let us read the Gospel, a small section each day. This way we will learn what is most essential in our lives: love and mercy.

Pope Francis @Pontifex • 25 August 2013

Don't be afraid to ask God for forgiveness. He never tires of forgiving us. God is pure mercy.

The world responds to this emphasis on mercy. Following his "Who am I to judge?" comments, Pope Francis found himself on the unlikeliest of magazine covers: *The Advocate,* a magazine for LGBT folks, with a "No H8" tattoo Photoshopped on his cheek. While Mass attendance hasn't spiked, Catholics of all stripes anecdotally report that they feel proud again talking about their faith publicly. Sure, there are those Catholics who see a cosmic battle between the Church and secular society, who abhor positive feelings from the popular culture toward the Church, because the Church should always be at odds with a corrupt culture. This isn't, however, the pope's view. Embrace culture, show some mercy, and help heal those who are hurting. That's this pope's message, in word, deed, and keystrokes. This message resonates with many Catholics because they know firsthand about the need for mercy. As any family knows, life is messy, and mercy, more so than judgment, is helpful in picking up the pieces.

Pope Francis @Pontifex • 19 September 2013

We are all sinners, but we experience the joy of God's forgiveness and we walk forward trusting in his mercy.

Pope Francis @Pontifex • 14 May 2015

Dear parents, have great patience, and forgive from the depths of your heart.

Still, there are many who feel excluded from this "Church of mercy." Divorced and remarried Catholics, for instance, are still unable to receive communion or serve as godparents, and many women feel that their gifts still aren't welcome in parishes and dioceses. Catholic gays and lesbians benefit from advances in the world at large, but many say they still can't find a home within their own church.

And then there are sinners—everyone, as Francis reminds us—who might feel too ashamed to be active in their faith community. My mistakes are too great, too embarrassing, we think. So some stay home, suffering. And, thus, the Church suffers, too. "This pains me," Francis said in a March 2015 homily. Francis asked those gathered at Mass how Jesus would treat someone ashamed of his or her sins, too embarrassed and cut off from their community. "Scold them because they are hurt? No, he comes and he carries them on his shoulders. And this is called mercy." Francis went on to lament that hurting Christians too often encounter not mercy, but "closed doors." He slammed those Christians who fail to recognize that God works through all kinds of people, so-called Christians, in other words, who slam shut the door to God's grace. "So, what the Holy Spirit creates in the hearts of people, those Christians with their 'doctors of the law' mentality, destroy."

Mercy, the pope believes, trumps legalism, exclusion, and purity. Or, as he put it to the International Congress on Catechesis, "I would prefer a thousand times over a bruised Church than an ill Church!"

 Pope Francis @Pontifex • 16 May 2015
It is better to have a Church that is wounded but out in the streets than a Church that is sick because it is closed in on itself.

A Church of mercy is a Church of sinners. That concerns those who want the Church to be filled with saints. But a pure Church has never been a reality, Francis reminds his followers. As he articulated in October 2013, Francis wants a Church that "calls everyone, welcomes them, is open even to those furthest from her." Francis's vision for the Church is "not a house for the few, but a house for everyone, where all can be renewed, transformed, sanctified by his love—the strongest and the weakest, sinners, the indifferent, those who feel discouraged or lost."

 Pope Francis @Pontifex • 17 August 2014
It is by God's mercy that we are saved. May we never tire of spreading this joyful message to the world.

The Francis Revolution, if it's successful, will rely on transforming the hearts and minds of individual believers. That's why the pope uses plain language, powerful images, and punchy Tweets to make his points. Lofty theological treatises have their place—and Francis is capable of writing them—but that's not how people learn, speak, or communicate today. At the center of Francis's Vatican is mercy. That's why Francis is making sure his bishops think about it as they deliberate sensitive issues about the family. It's why he exhorts priests "to smell of sheep" and be with their people. And it's why he Tweets so often about mercy to his followers. It's a message aimed mostly at everyday Catholics. If we live more merciful lives, in accordance not just with Francis's hopes but with the Gospels themselves, the Church will be renewed as well. This is the impetus for Francis's Year of Mercy, a special jubilee year launched at the end of 2015 during which believers are reminded again and again that God's grace and mercy are more powerful than any of our sins or shortcomings. Francis truly believes mercy is the Lord's greatest gift and he wants to share this realization with his followers. The only question remaining is, have we got on board?

4

Suffering

During a visit to the Philippines in early 2015, Francis was moved by the suffering so many children experience in this deeply Catholic country. Even as a tropical storm bore down on Manila, nearly thirty thousand young people braved the elements, intent on securing a spot to hear the pope deliver his talk.

Filipinos were still reeling from Typhoon Haiyan, which had killed more than six thousand and left millions displaced and homeless, just over a year earlier. While life in Manila can be difficult for many, children especially suffer here, with as many as 1.2 million living in poverty.

Pope Francis @Pontifex • 11 November 2013

We remember the Philippines, Vietnam and the entire region hit by Typhoon Haiyan. Please be generous with prayers and concrete help.

Twelve-year-old Glyzelle Palomar broke down in tears as she asked Pope Francis a question, one of a handful of kids chosen to reflect on life as a young person here. Rescued from the streets, Palomar had seen lots of children suffering, and she wanted to know why God allowed it to happen. "Many children get involved in drugs and prostitution," she said. "Why does God allow these things to happen to us? The children are not guilty of anything."

Francis was visibly shaken. He laid aside his prepared remarks and spoke in Spanish, his native tongue. A priest translated his remarks into English for the crowd. "Deep down," Francis told the girl, the question "is almost unanswerable." But for forty minutes, he tried his best to make some sense of all the suffering.

 Pope Francis @Pontifex • 1 January 2015

How many innocent people and children suffer in the world! Lord, grant us your peace!

The pope noticed that the girl had been crying when she asked her question. He praised this. "Only when we are able to weep over the things that you experienced, can we understand and give some kind of response. . . . Why do children suffer? Only when our hearts can ask this question and weep can we begin to understand."

He explained that weeping in the face of suffering is one way to acknowledge that suffering is real, not something to be swept under the rug. We need to stand in the face of suffering and let it sink in, stir our imaginations. In the face of great suffering, offering the equivalent of a single coin isn't enough. As Christians, we're called to do more. But before we act, we have to reflect on the suffering we encounter. Jesus didn't cure a few sick folks and call it a day. It was only when Jesus paused to weep "did he understand our troubles," the pope said. Francis praised people who know how to weep, including the marginalized, the neglected, and the scorned. "Those of us who have relatively comfortable lives, we don't know how to weep," he said. And as a result, we often don't know how to act.

The world needs to weep in the face of suffering, as "certain realities of life are seen only with eyes that are cleansed by tears." Francis asked those listening to learn to see the world through tears: "Can I weep when I see a child who is hungry, on drugs and on the street, homeless, abandoned, mistreated or exploited as a slave by society?"

Pope Francis @Pontifex • 12 July 2013

Lord, grant us the grace to weep over our indifference, over the cruelty that is in the world and in ourselves.

Pope Francis doesn't try to explain why bad things happen to people on Twitter. That's a question that would take more than 140 characters to answer. He Tweets about suffering, however, as it's a part of being human, and something the Church must find ways to address. He asks his followers to respond in two ways. First, we should resist the temptation to avoid any encounter with suffering. We should acknowledge suffering, and let it move us. The second response is taking action, walking alongside those who hurt. Francis wants us to slow down and spend time with those suffering physically, mentally, and spirituality. His Tweets call us to engage with concrete acts of love and charity. Reflect, pray, and act: this is the pope's Twitter formula for so many topics, including suffering.

We may not understand the vexing conundrum of suffering any better as a result of the pope's Tweets, but he reminds us that Christians are called to show love, care, and concern to those in need. Francis wants the Church to accompany people through all stages of life. This means accepting that some parts of life will be darker than others. In the process, we might learn to see the world in a new light when we respond with love.

Pope Francis @Pontifex • 30 December 2014

Today people are suffering from poverty, but also from lack of love.

Pope Francis @Pontifex • 24 March 2015

Suffering is a call to conversion: it reminds us of our frailty and vulnerability.

Pope Francis @Pontifex • 10 April 2014

Jesus teaches us to not be ashamed of touching human misery, of touching his flesh in our brothers and sisters who suffer. (EG 270)

Pope Francis often uses his Twitter account to bring attention to disasters and situations that cause suffering.

Pope Francis @Pontifex • 21 May 2013

I am close to the families of all who died in the Oklahoma tornado, especially those who lost young children. Join me in praying for them.

Pope Francis @Pontifex • 19 April 2014

Please join me in praying for the victims of the ferry disaster in Korea and their families.

 Pope Francis @Pontifex • 27 January 2015

Auschwitz cries out with the pain of immense suffering and pleads for a future of respect, peace and encounter among peoples.

Some say these Tweets about suffering open the pope to charges of "slacktivism." This is the term used to describe those who affirm a cause through social media with the only result being the ego gratification of the "slacktivist" while making no real contribution to the cause. It doesn't take much effort to Tweet out a caring thought, but what difference does it really make? If Francis stopped only at highlighting the various ways in which people suffer, maybe he'd be guilty of slacktivism. But there's a second part to Francis's Tweets, and that's getting his followers to allow themselves to be moved by suffering so that they respond with love.

Once we weep, we'll have a better sense of how to respond. It's in that response where we'll find God. If we shrug with indifference when we encounter suffering, we're forsaking our Christian responsibility to care for those in need. Francis wants the Church to be a community of mercy, compassion, and charity. Those seemingly abstract values must be manifested in concrete acts.

 Pope Francis @Pontifex • 20 June 2014

There is so much indifference in the face of suffering. May we overcome indifference with concrete acts of charity.

Suffering is one of the great mysteries of Christian life, "a condition of life on earth from which no one is spared," as he said in May 2014. It's not a sign that God has abandoned those who suffer, but quite the opposite.

 Pope Francis @Pontifex • 17 February 2014

To all who are sick, do not lose hope, especially when your suffering is at its worst Christ is near you.

 Pope Francis @Pontifex • 17 January 2015

The com-passion of God, his suffering-with-us, gives meaning and worth to our struggles and our sufferings.

Pope Francis @Pontifex • 21 March 2014

Sickness and death are not taboo subjects. They are realities that we must face in Jesus' presence.

Suffering, while by no means good in and of itself, can nevertheless open our eyes to a new way of seeing life. This view of suffering isn't a "sadomasochistic attitude," as Francis memorably put it. Suffering isn't pleasant, something to seek out for its own sake. Francis believes our response to suffering is an opportunity to see God in our lives. Accompanying others through their difficult moments is one of the most basic of Christian tasks, and Francis reminds us that spending time with those who suffer is a chance to encounter God as well.

"Time spent with the sick is holy time," Francis said in his message for the 2015 World Day of the Sick, an antidote to the craziness of daily life. "Occasionally our world forgets the special value of time spent at the bedside of the sick, since we are in such a rush; caught up as we are in a frenzy of doing, of producing," he said, "we forget about giving ourselves freely, taking care of others, being responsible for others." All people are called to this kind of encounter, and if we avoid standing with the suffering, not in the abstract but with actual people, our humanity is diminished and we miss what God seeks to teach us.

Pope Francis @Pontifex • 5 January 2015

Lord, help us to recognize you in the sick, poor and suffering.

Pope Francis envisions a Church in which believers encounter one another and spend time caring for one another where we are. This means accepting that suffering is in some fashion an inevitable part of life. The pope's notion that God's goodness is to be found among the suffering might seem odd at first glance. Elsewhere in this book, I highlight the pope's concerns for some groups particularly prone to suffering, such as the elderly, the disabled, the young, migrants. Pope Francis seeks to shape how we respond to their particular challenges, as well as individuals in our families and faith communities dealing with other difficulties. He wants us to meet people where they are, which sometimes means embracing their suffering, and to respond with love. Francis is trying to mold a Church of mercy. It's only when we acknowledge that suffering is a reality that this is truly possible.

5

Gossip

THE FIGHT AGAINST GOSSIP HASN'T DRIVEN THIS PAPACY, BUT Francis has Tweeted about it a couple of times. I decided to include it as a chapter because while it is not a major theme of the pope's agenda, it is still an important one. I thought it also allows us a window into how the pope's activity on Twitter works in conjunction with his more official work and efforts.

Gossip is one of those daily temptations we all succumb to once in a while. Francis doesn't want us to feel guilty about it, but he thinks we should avoid it when possible. It's bad for families, workplaces, and communities, and when it gets out of control, it's catastrophic for the Church as a whole. Francis is trying to get his bishops to stop gossiping. It's just not very Christian, and it threatens the kind of Church Francis envisions: merciful, welcoming, and one capable of showing God's love. Gossip is also of personal concern to this pope. While he's beloved by most Catholics, there are a few important churchmen not on board with his agenda, and sometimes they resort to gossip to undercut him.

Francis is immensely popular in the United States. A Pew Research Center poll taken to mark the second anniversary of his election found that 95 percent of all church-going Catholics in the United States hold a favorable view on him. Those numbers are on a par with the wildly beloved Pope John Paul II, even at the height of his popularity throughout most of the 1990s. Like we read in the first chapter, across the world, it's the same story: majorities in Europe (84 percent), the United States (78 percent), and Latin America (72 percent) hold favorable views of Francis. The pope's popularity cuts across political divides, age groups, and even believers of other faiths and those with no faith, with 70 percent of those with no religious affiliation holding a favorable view of the pope.

But inside the Church, things aren't as rosy for Francis.

When Pope Benedict XVI retired, the Roman Curia—the pope's cabinet of cardinals and bishops that effectively runs the institutional Church—was in crisis. Rumors of kickbacks and questionable financial deals abounded. Benedict's own butler betrayed him, releasing internal documents to the media that revealed just how out of whack things had gotten. In the days leading up to the papal conclave in March 2013, the cardinals charged with choosing the next pope knew something had to give. The Vatican needed an outsider, someone unafraid to shake things up and get the Church's house in order. That man, of course, was Pope Francis.

Elected as a reformer at the age of seventy-six, Pope Francis ascended the papal throne knowing he didn't have much time to make a difference. So he moved quickly, creating new offices to manage the Vatican's unwieldy financial situation. He limited the power of the Curia by establishing a group of nine cardinal advisors who meet regularly to guide his work. And he clipped the wings of powerful opponents who seek to derail his efforts.

But being men of God, these suddenly marginalized cardinals and bishops swallowed their pride and fell in line behind Francis, their new leader. Not quite. Rather than going along with Francis, some launched a whisper campaign, which included plenty of gossip and second-guessing, in order to undercut the pope's reforms. The innuendo, rumors, and outright lies some Church leaders have leaked to the media would make even the most vicious "mean girl" blush. One of Francis's key Vatican Bank appointees was accused of carrying on an illicit gay relationship. Later, during the Synod on the Family, bishops sympathetic to liberal reforms in the Church were accused of prematurely releasing a synod report with language friendly to gays and the divorced and remarried to skew the debate. Others suggested that the Vatican mail room was in on the conspiracy, not delivering copies of books defending current Church teaching to synod participants. When the pope's financial reforms were kicking into high gear, his point man on money was subject to rumors that he had spent lavishly on office decor and vestments. Gossip was rampant, aimed at undercutting Francis's allies.

One prominent cardinal working in the Vatican, an American, became something of a champion for those doubting the pope's leadership. He said that "many" people had expressed their "concerns" over Pope Francis. "There is a strong sense that the church is like a ship without a rudder," he said in an October 30 interview with the Spanish Catholic newspaper *Vida Nueva*. He said he didn't share those feelings personally, but by attributing them to someone else, he made sure the pope's critics knew they had a powerful ally in Rome. It would be short lived. About a week later he was sacked from his role as head of the Vatican's highest court, assigned to a largely ceremonial role as chaplain to the Knights of Malta. This particular case is the most extreme—a powerful cardinal publicly questioning the pope's leadership only to lose his post shortly thereafter—but he's not alone.

A bishop in the United States said Francis was turning off conservative Catholics. Another cardinal questioned if the pope really understood how his speeches and homilies were being received in the wider world. And many priests and lay Catholics continue to experience a certain discomfort each time Francis sets aside his prepared texts, speaks from his heart, and generates new headlines. Some in the Vatican think the best way to resist the pope's changes is to leak stories and innuendo—usually of the financial and moral kind—that could take out the pope's key allies. These kinds of tactics are often used by clerics intent on preserving their own power and prestige, sometimes at the expense of promoting the Gospel. Francis has a message for those bishops: cut it out.

The pope's Tweets about gossip are "Easter eggs," those hidden gems I described in the first chapter that really only make total sense to those who know what they're looking for. There are just a couple that directly address gossip, but by understanding what's going on behind the scenes, they pack a lot more punch than we might assume. Francis wants his bishops to stop obsessing about their own power and prestige, and get out into the world. Halting gossip is one of the first steps toward this goal. But he isn't Tweeting about gossip just to get his troops in line (though undoubtedly that's a nice side effect). Rather, he wants individual believers to mirror Jesus more closely, and gossip is something that pulls us further away. The Francis Revolution won't come about with dramatic changes in Church teaching or with the sale of priceless Vatican art to open soup kitchens. Instead, the Francis Revolution will come when individual believers start living more like Jesus, from the ordinary Catholic in the pew all the way to the highest-ranking cardinal in the Curia.

 Pope Francis @Pontifex • 9 June 2014

May we never talk about others behind their backs, but speak to them openly about what we think.

When he elevated new cardinals in 2014, the pope urged those gathered inside Saint Peter's Basilica to resist the temptations that come along with being a prince of the Church, most notably trying to consolidate their own power like a zero-sum game. Whisper campaigns can be good for that sort of thing, and Francis isn't naive. During his homily to the new cardinals, he said, "A cardinal enters the Church of Rome, not a royal court. . . . May all of us avoid, and help others to avoid, habits and ways of acting typical of a court: intrigue, gossip, cliques, favoritism and preferences." While those vices are hardly exclusive to the Church—a quick glance at a newspaper shows that all corridors of power are ripe for the same sorts of nastiness—Francis begged his cardinals not to give in to the temptation. But he had his work cut out for him. Francis knows that getting the Church back to the basics will require the transformation of many hearts, and putting a halt to nasty gossip is an important benchmark toward that end.

Fans of Francis praise his encouragement of conversation and debate in the Church, even on controversial topics such as women, contraception, divorce, and sexuality. These issues took center stage at the Synod on the Family, a yearlong meeting launched in October 2014. But for bishops and lay Catholics who have toed the line the last few decades—in the Church as well as in the public square—this shake-up is hard to take. For the first time in a long time, the Church was asking itself tough questions, recognizing that the realities many families face today aren't receiving adequate pastoral care in parishes. Should divorced and remarried Catholics be allowed to receive communion? Should parishes be more welcoming to gay couples? What about the role of women in the Church? Prominent cardinals on each side of the debate sniped back and forth in the press, accusing each side of using underhanded means to advance their cause. Each morning, as they entered the Synod Hall, cardinals and bishops would address the press pool, providing fresh drama. A Tweet Francis sent in the midst of all this drama showed he knew what was going on, and wanted his men to knock it off:

Pope Francis @Pontifex • 7 October 2014

Let us ask the Lord for the grace not to speak badly of others, not to criticize, not to gossip, but rather to love everyone.

About thirty thousand people re-Tweeted and favorited the Tweet. More than a handful of cardinals and bishops, it seems, probably weren't among them.

A few months later, days before the pope was set to announce changes to the Vatican departments that handle finances, someone leaked receipts showing how much money the pope's point man on money, Cardinal George Pell of Australia, had spent decorating his own office and buying new vestments. Stories flooded the Catholic press. Detractors suggested that one of the pope's own men wasn't falling in line behind the frugal pope. The intent was clear: undermine the pope, derail his reforms, and keep things the way they've been. Even though the pope rules with hardly any checks, the reality is that the way his decisions are reported in the press has a huge impact. If everyday Catholics aren't on board, a pope can be rendered impotent. The bishops trying to question the pope's leadership knew this and were happy to contribute to the skepticism— not a very Christian response by those who felt threatened by the Francis Revolution.

"Who am I to judge?"—perhaps the most famous line ever uttered by Francis—is the result of gossip,

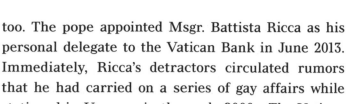

too. The pope appointed Msgr. Battista Ricca as his personal delegate to the Vatican Bank in June 2013. Immediately, Ricca's detractors circulated rumors that he had carried on a series of gay affairs while stationed in Uruguay in the early 2000s. The Vatican denied the allegations. On his return flight from Rio in July, the pope was asked about gay priests. "Who am I to judge?" he replied. Ricca kept his job, which sent a strong and undeniable message to all of the Vatican's gossipmongers: the old ways won't work anymore.

The old ways, the pope believes, stifle conversation and even keep the Holy Spirit at bay. Bishops and laypeople were afraid to speak up, to voice disagreement, for fear of retribution or slander. Francis wants that to change, so he's encouraged those who disagree with him to say so, honestly and respectfully. Francis can handle dissent, but he won't tolerate gossip.

In his 2014 Christmas address to Vatican employees, an update usually used to thank them for a year of hard work, Pope Francis zeroed in on what he called the "spiritual ailments" plaguing the Church. They included the "terrorism of gossip," used to "kill the reputation of our colleagues and brothers in cold blood." The crowd, anticipating a more merry address, applauded tepidly. Francis went on. "It's the sickness of cowardly people who, not having the courage to speak directly, talk behind people's backs." This pope isn't a shrinking violet. He knows the bully pulpit is among his most powerful tools, and he's not afraid to use it, in person and on Twitter.

Of course, gossip doesn't just plague cardinals and bishops. The pope's words apply to everyday Catholics, too. Francis devoted much of a Wednesday general audience in early 2014 to the theme, telling the crowd gathered below him in Saint Peter's Square that engaging in gossip is a sure way to derail a path to holiness. "I am convinced that if each one of us would purposely avoid gossip, at the end, we would become a saint! It's a beautiful path!" Francis acknowledged the allure of gossip, a pastime that "seems to be something enjoyable and fun, like a piece of candy." But, like too many sweets, he said, gossip eventually "fills the heart with bitterness and also poisons us." Reflecting on the Gospel reading from that day, in which Jesus tells his followers that anger harbored toward another person is tantamount to committing violence against them, Francis made sure not to mince words: "Gossip," he made clear, "can also kill, because it kills the reputation of the person."

Christians should be known by their love for one another, but sometimes it seems we're no different than the rest of the world, gossip included. Francis wants us to stop.

Francis headed down to Naples in March 2015, this time to speak to the heads of religious communities. Anyone who's spent any time in a monastery knows that, sometimes, gossip thrives there. Francis suggested that the presence of gossip in a community is a sure sign of sickness. "For me there is a sign that there is no fraternity in the presbyterate or in religious communities. The sign is gossip, the terrorism of gossip," he said. A person who gossips, the pope continued, "is a terrorist who drops a bomb, destroys, and they are outside . . . they did a kamikaze . . . they destroy others." "Gossip is terrorism" is a powerful message. Francis speaks like he Tweets, using memorable phrases that are short and to the point, and that pack a punch. That's why he's such a natural for Twitter: many of his best Tweets are lines straight out of his speeches. He knows that most Catholics don't have the time to read his every word, so he can pick out the key points and communicate with them directly in just a few seconds.

Francis has used this idea of gossip as a weapon frequently. He called it a "criminal" act, one akin to murder, in September 2013, saying the source of that teaching is God. He wanted to make sure he got the message through: "There is no place for nuances. If you speak ill of your brother, you kill your brother. And every time we do this, we are imitating that gesture of Cain, the first murderer in history."

Gossip isn't rare in the world, and that's the point. It's a tactic, Francis believes, that should be beneath Christians. For too long, ladder-climbing priests and bishops used gossip as another weapon in their arsenal to attain a more prestigious job, a higher office. This is at odds with the Gospel, and Francis has made it a mission to weed out gossip in the Church.

But what about people who can't resist the temptation to gossip? Ever the pastor, Francis offered some ideas. Before slandering another person, Christians who have a beef with another person should first pray about it, and then confront the other person face-to-face. "Go and pray for him! Go and do penance for her! And then, if it is necessary, speak to that person who may be able to seek remedy for the problem," he said. He did just this in November 2013, telephoning a writer who had published an article critical of the pope. The pope's spiritual advice on how to deal with gossip, how to live more like Jesus, doesn't take too many keystrokes to communicate.

In December 2013, Francis offered some very practical advice warning against gossip in another message seemingly ready-made for Twitter: "Always greet people nicely, always with a smile."

While Francis has Tweeted about gossip just a couple of times, his messages clearly communicate his feelings. Christians need to stop sniping and get back to the Gospel.

6

Welcome

WHEN POPE FRANCIS TWEETS TO THE WORLD, HE KNOWS HIS audience is comprised of the people who can take his vision for the Church and run with it. Without buy-in from everyday Catholics—who comprise the vast majority of the Church—the pope's ability to have a lasting impact is rather limited. It would be back to business as usual once his papacy is over, and he's acknowledged on more than one occasion that he's not going to be pope for very long. So it's up to his followers—virtual and otherwise—to make his vision a reality. A major part of that vision involves reshaping the attitude and culture of the whole Church, from Saint Peter's down to the smallest rural parish. Francis is a pope of mercy, and he wants the Church to be a living reality of this virtue. To achieve this, Francis is pushing Catholics to create a more welcoming

Church, one confident in the belief that God's love and forgiveness are meant to be shared with all.

It would not come as a surprise to many Catholics that the Church is sometimes perceived as more judgmental than its founder intended. Jesus palled around with prostitutes, tax collectors, and other dregs of society. He sought out those whom society had no use for, and welcomed them into his fold. A couple thousand years later, Catholic parishes sometimes come across less as a collection of castoffs and more as a country club for the righteous. Francis wants this to change. He exhorts Catholics to extend a welcome to those who need it most: sinners, failures, those whom life has beaten up a bit. The truth is at some point in everyone's life, these labels will apply. Francis hopes we remember that, and live our faith accordingly.

 Pope Francis @Pontifex • 28 April 2015

Every Christian community must be a welcoming home for those searching for God, for those searching for a brother or sister to listen to them.

 Pope Francis @Pontifex • 16 June 2013

Let the Church always be a place of mercy and hope, where everyone is welcomed, loved and forgiven.

Pope Francis @Pontifex • 2 December 2014

The Church is called to draw near to every person, beginning with the poorest and those who suffer.

Even when he was a cardinal, Francis preferred the quiet life of a pastor, largely eschewing the perks that come along with being a prince of the Church. This is why he knows firsthand the challenges the Church faces in addressing modern pastoral needs, and why some perceive the Church to be less than welcoming.

As pope, he recalled hearing about a "very sad little girl" in Buenos Aires who confided to her teacher that her melancholy was due to the mother's fiancé not liking her. It was one of those messy life situations of which Francis has the courage to acknowledge instead of sweeping aside or speaking about only in hushed tones. He noted that this situation was not unique in Argentina, one of several "challenges that sometimes are difficult to understand." Given that life can be so messy, Francis posed a question to those gathered, and indeed to all Catholics and those interested in his thoughts: "How can we proclaim Christ to a generation that is changing?" With the question, he added a warning: "We must be careful not to administer a vaccine against faith." The Church must be a place of refuge for all people. That's a message the pope has posted on Twitter again and again, highlighting his homilies and speeches that often convey a similar sentiment.

Pope Francis @Pontifex • 30 November 2013

The Church invites everyone to be embraced by the Father's tenderness and forgiveness.

Pope Francis @Pontifex • 25 April 2015

We Christians are called to go out of ourselves to bring the mercy and tenderness of God to all.

Pope Francis @Pontifex • 15 November 2014

A Christian brings peace to others. Not only peace, but also love, kindness, faithfulness and joy.

Why is the Church perceived as unwelcoming? One of the challenges in creating a welcoming Church, Francis believes, is a fear of scandal, of breaking the rules. If we are soft on the rules and beliefs of the Church, the thinking goes, we compromise the truth. That is why Francis Tweets about God's love and mercy on a regular basis. Truth is truth, but we must start with love and mercy, just as God does with us. Our sinfulness is not bigger than God. But opening the Church doors and posting an "All Are Welcome" sign are not enough. A hallmark of a welcoming Church is having the courage to believe that God's love is meant for all, and then going out and inviting others to experience love and mercy.

 Pope Francis @Pontifex • 14 September 2013

Sometimes it is possible to live without knowing our neighbours: this is not Christian.

 Pope Francis @Pontifex • 2 August 2013

The security of faith does not make us motionless or close us off, but sends us forth to bear witness and to dialogue with all people.

Francis has said he is a "son of the Church," and thus he hasn't altered a single rule. But he is especially aware that just because he thinks all the Church's beliefs and rituals are true and correct, the Church still faces serious challenges in bringing hope to people's lives. The crisis facing the Church is due more to its image in the world than to its doctrines. In other words, if the Church's rules, beliefs, and rituals are lived out in ways that make those coming to church feel they aren't welcome, the pope sees a problem.

In February 2015, Francis elevated twenty new cardinals, many from the peripheries of the Church.

He used the consistory Mass to preach about the need for these princes of the Church to create a more welcoming environment. He spoke bluntly about opening up the Church: Jesus wants the Church to be welcoming and who are we to question him? To help make his case, he reflected on Jesus healing the leper.

Despite the law prohibiting him to do so, "Jesus responds immediately to the leper's plea, without waiting to study the situation and all its possible consequences." Jesus is concerned not with legalisms, but with "reaching out to save those far off, healing the wounds of the sick, restoring everyone to God's family," Francis said. "He does not think of the closed-minded who are scandalized even by a work of healing, scandalized before any kind of openness, by any action outside of their mental and spiritual boxes, by any caress or sign of tenderness which does not fit into their usual thinking and their ritual purity." Francis wants the Church to be a refuge for all, especially those who might not seem a natural fit at first glance. That's how Jesus rolled, after all.

Later that year, Francis preached to the heads of religious communities meeting in Rome. He recalled his days in Buenos Aires, where he worked with people who didn't feel welcome in the Church. He put aside his prepared remarks and decided to answer questions from the audience instead. Someone asked the pope, what should the Church emphasize today? Well, Francis said, the Church must be "attractive. Wake up the world! Be witnesses of a different way of doing things, of acting, of living!"

The phrase "Wake up the world!" is a wonderful example of a "Francis-ism": short, to the point, and still inspiring. It's a rallying cry for his millions of followers and the Church at large. "Life is complicated," he continued, "it consists of grace and sin."

The Tweets Francis sends are re-Tweeted tens of thousands of times, so the number of people reading his short messages easily climbs well into the millions. But it doesn't stop there. Because Francis is expert at articulating the Gospel in fresh and pithy ways, countless others Tweet his words, further extending the Francis Revolution via Twitter. When Francis says things like "Wake up the world!" his followers jump into action. Even though he didn't Tweet that phrase out himself, it's as if Francis speaks in clips ready-made for Twitter. He truly is the Tweetable pope.

Among the most famous Francis lines is "Who am I to judge?" (widely Tweeted by almost everyone, it seemed, except the pope), the pope's reply to a reporter who asked him about gay priests. Progressive Catholics have rallied around the rhetorical question as a sign that Francis wants the doors to the Church thrown open to all those who have felt marginalized. There's certainly some truth to that interpretation. During the controversial Synod on the Family in October 2014, cardinals and bishops debated if parishes should be more welcoming to gays and lesbians, a debate unimaginable even a decade ago. Francis acknowledged a few months later in *La Nacion* that the Church and its leaders must consider how to support "a family that has a homosexual son or daughter."

On the issue of Catholics who divorce and remarry, who are in violation of Church law, Francis has lamented what he sees as their "de facto excommunication." He's pushed bishops to consider ways to "open the doors a little bit more" to them, perhaps even allowing them to receive communion.

When it comes to the role of women in the Church, the pope has had some hiccups. He's joked about overbearing mothers-in-law and housekeepers, he's made unflattering references to "spinsters" and the infertile, and he once called women theologians on a papal commission the "strawberries on the cake." For the sake of argument, those comments can be chalked up to Francis being old enough to be a grandfather, coming from an earlier time and place.

Much more frequently, however, he's spoken about the need for women to feel welcome, even if their ordination is off the table. "I am convinced of the urgency of offering spaces for women in the Church and to welcome them," he said in February 2015. He said he hoped to see "many women involved in pastoral responsibilities, in the accompaniment of persons, families and groups, as well as in theological reflection."

In addition to single moms, gays, women, and the divorced and remarried, the welcoming Church

Francis envisions includes a whole slew of characters who have not always felt at home in the Church.

There are the homeless, for example, some of whom were given a private tour of the Sistine Chapel, Vatican Museums, and gardens. Francis stopped by to say hello and shake hands. "Welcome," he said. "This is everyone's house, and your house. The doors are always open for all."

 Pope Francis @Pontifex • 31 May 2013

The whole of salvation history is the story of God looking for us: he offers us love and welcomes us with tenderness.

Because of his experience living among the people in Buenos Aires, Francis knows life is messy. And he also knows there are a lot more people out there who live out this reality each day. More than 21 million of them follow him on Twitter, so it's no wonder he Tweets so frequently about the need for the Church to be a welcoming place. Francis wants to share the good news of God's love with as many people as possible, and he knows that making people feel welcome is the first step. "The Church's doors must be open so that all may come and that we can go out of those doors and proclaim the Gospel," he preached in June 2013.

An unwelcoming community, on the other hand, is toxic for believers. "When the Church closes in on itself," he warned in June 2014, "when it thinks of itself as a 'school of religion,' with so many great ideas, with many beautiful temples, with many fine museums, with many beautiful things, but does not give witness, it becomes sterile."

 Pope Francis @Pontifex • 29 May 2013

The Church is born from the supreme act of love on the Cross, from Jesus' open side. The Church is a family where we love and are loved.

Francis is keenly aware that life is messy. But he also knows that people hunger for love and acceptance. He wants the Church to be that space for as many people as possible. "Total openness to serving others is our hallmark," he said at the Mass with new cardinals. "It alone is our title of honor." Of course, that statement was aspirational, like so much of what Francis says. A pope who is a master communicator, he offered the new cardinals this bit of wisdom: "Contact is the true language of communication." Go, be with people, and make them feel welcome. For someone who's hurting, often the last thing they need to hear is judgment. Francis believes that mercy is a much better salve for the soul. If he can convince several million Catholics on Twitter to take him up on this challenge, his legacy will last far longer than his papacy, and the Church will be better off for it.

7

Creation

AFTER MONTHS OF ANTICIPATION AND RANCOROUS DEBATE about what he would and would not say about the environment, Pope Francis released *Laudato Si'*, or Praise Be to You. In this first encyclical devoted to the environment, Francis blamed "unfettered greed" for pollution, inequality, and global warming, which he accepted "mainly as a result of human activity," sparking a wave of protest among climate change skeptics. The pope linked the damage human beings have caused to the environment with the plight of the poor, remarking that a changing environment's "worst impact will probably be felt by developing countries in coming decades."

The sprawling encyclical, one of the highest forms of Church teaching, touched on a variety of topics, challenging the left and the right on how it approaches the issue. To think the free market and technology alone can save the planet is ludicrous, the pope wrote, and so is the idea that there are too many people on earth, that we need population control in order to live in harmony with the planet. In short, the encyclical calls for immediate action from policy makers and individual believers, stating quite simply that the Earth is beginning "to look more and more like an immense pile of filth." If you think that kind of sharp message sounds perfect for Twitter, you're not alone.

The morning the encyclical was released, June 18, 2015, I was at the Vatican covering the press conference, historical in itself. Joining a Catholic cardinal to unveil the document was an Orthodox theologian, an atheist scientist, and a Catholic laywoman who leads one of the Church's largest global antipoverty nonprofits. The message was clear: cleaning up the environment is a task that will take all of us working together. Before it began, I was given a heads-up to listen for some exciting Twitter news. Finally, at the end of the nearly two-hour event, the Vatican's spokesperson announced that to help spread the pope's teaching, Francis would utilize a "Twitterbomb," a slang term describing the publication of several Tweets in a row about one topic to attract attention. So for the next twenty-four hours, @Pontifex Tweeted highlights from *Laudato Si'*.

Pope Francis @Pontifex • 18 June 2015

There is an intimate relationship between the poor and the fragility of the planet. #LaudatoSi

 Pope Francis @Pontifex • 18 June 2015

Climate change represents one of the principal challenges facing humanity in our day. #LaudatoSi

Pope Francis @Pontifex • 18 June 2015

The earth, our home, is beginning to look more and more like an immense pile of filth.

By the end of the "Twitterbomb," Francis published more than sixty Tweets about the encyclical, by far the highest number of Tweets devoted to a single cause in such a short period of time. There's no question that the environment is important to this pope. But it didn't begin with his Twitterbomb.

Six days after the conclave that elected him pope, Francis celebrated his inaugural Mass in Saint Peter's Square, which happened to be the feast day of Saint Joseph. During the homily, Francis explored Joseph's role as "protector" of Mary, Jesus, and the Church, and said that that saint's example serves as a model for all Christians. (The pope's admiration for the relatively unknown Joseph manifested itself again in his June 2013 decision to alter the language of the Mass to include prayers to Joseph during the Eucharistic prayer.) Joseph is an effective protector, Francis said, because "he can look at things realistically, he is in touch with his surroundings, he can make truly wise decisions." Francis exhorted those listening to emulate Joseph the protector and "protect Christ in our lives, so that we can protect others, so that we can protect creation!" Like we read in chapter 1, he then Tweeted out a synopsis of his homily that has guided his papacy ever since.

 Pope Francis @Pontifex • 19 March 2013
Let us keep a place for Christ in our lives, let us care for one another and let us be loving custodians of creation.

Perhaps Francis was taking a cue from his predecessor, Pope Benedict XVI, who consistently showed his concern for the environment in both word and deed. Benedict frequently spoke about the need for developed nations to step up to fight climate change, and he even installed solar panels at the Vatican and launched a carbon-offset initiative to make the Holy See the first carbon-neutral state. (That the effort ultimately failed, victim to the mismanagement on the part of the firm the Vatican hired, is a sad example of the many good intentions Benedict championed but was unable to implement because of inept bureaucrats, both inside the Church and out.)

During the homily, Francis took advantage of his global stage to issue a call to action to all people, not just Catholics. Being a protector, he said, "is simply human, involving everyone. It means protecting all creation, the beauty of the created world, as the Book of Genesis tells us and as Saint Francis of Assisi showed us." Francis tied safeguarding the environment to protecting the marginalized, "especially children, the elderly, those in need, who are often the last we think about."

Francis said there are consequences for failing to live up to our calling as protectors: "whenever we fail to care for creation and for our brothers and sisters, the way is opened for destruction, and hearts are hardened." He likened those who disregard the plight of the planet and the poor to "Herods who plot death, wreak havoc, and mar the countenance of men and women." He begged those "who have positions of responsibility in economic, political, and social life, and all men and women of goodwill" to be "protectors of one another and the environment." Responding to creation and to one another "with tenderness and love" is "to open up a horizon of hope," he said. "It is to let a shaft of light break through the heavy clouds; it is to bring the warmth of hope!"

Francis concluded his homily by stating, quite simply in a style now famously his, his charge as Bishop of Rome: "to protect Jesus with Mary, to protect the whole of creation, to protect each person, especially the poorest, to protect ourselves."

Though an ambitious call from the world's newest moral leader, Francis's call to protect creation was surprisingly accessible. Francis speaks in ways that cut through the noise. While his messages are short and to the point, they don't lack thoughtfulness or depth. That's why his words work so well on Twitter, staccato microhomilies perfect for our busy lives.

 Pope Francis @Pontifex • 21 April 2015

We need to care for the earth so that it may continue, as God willed, to be a source of life for the entire human family.

A month after his election, in a conversation with the president of Ecuador, Francis noted that care for creation was also one of the main concerns of his namesake, Francis of Assisi. While Francis chose his name based on his concern for the poor, more than a little of the thirteenth-century Italian saint's love for nature has seemed to rub off on the pope, too. "Take good care of creation," Francis told the president. "Saint Francis wanted that. People occasionally forgive, but nature never does. If we don't take care of the environment, there's no way of getting around it." Hardly a month has gone by since his election that Pope Francis has not made a bold statement about the need for Christians to protect the environment, a sign of its importance to this pope.

Climate change activists are keen on reminding the world that the effects of a changing earth—rising seas, hotter summers, and more intense storms—will impact the poor much more than the rich, individuals and nations alike. That appears to be at least one reason Francis is so emphatic on the issue, and he stated as much in June 2013 during his weekly general audience to pilgrims gathered in Saint Peter's Square. This prompted another gentle Twitter reminder that protecting creation is the responsibility of all Christians.

 Pope Francis @Pontifex • 5 June 2013

Care of creation is not just something God spoke of at the dawn of history: he entrusts it to each of us as part of his plan.

"We are living through a moment of crisis," Francis said in the June address, once again connecting the plight of the environment to the disregard for the poor and marginalized, tying both issues to what he termed our "throwaway culture." He asked the crowd, "Are we truly cultivating and protecting creation, or are we instead exploiting and neglecting it?" His answer, of course, was no, we are not protecting creation. Worse, he said, "we have distanced ourselves from God" and are "losing the attitude of wonder, of contemplation, of listening to creation." Because this "throwaway culture" is so pervasive, "men and women are sacrificed to the idols of money and consumption," often "thrown away, as if we were trash." For Francis, our response to God's love for creation, including human beings and the planet, determines our future. Human beings must resist the temptation to master and dominate creation and one another.

Speaking to another massive crowd gathered at Saint Peter's in the spring of 2014, Francis cut through the static that so often dominates the conversation about climate change and the environment. Though only May, the temperature in Rome had skyrocketed to the mid-80s, the beginning of what would be another dangerously hot European summer. Francis put it bluntly in a speech in May 2014: "Safeguard creation. Because if we destroy creation, creation will destroy us! Never forget this!" At just 96 characters, Francis again proved why he is the Tweetable pope, able to mobilize consciences with just a few sharp words.

He denounced those who erroneously believe that human beings can become "masters of creation," urging the crowd instead to be "custodians of creation." The created world is not meant to be privately held, but to be guarded as a "wonderful gift that God has given us, so that we care for it and we use it for the benefit of all." Again, he offered a message that was Twitter-ready: God always forgives. We sometimes forgive. Creation never forgives.

Later that year, in a letter to a group of climate change activists meeting in Lima, Peru, Francis tried to add a sense of urgency to his message. "The time to find global solutions is running out," he wrote. "We can find adequate solutions only if we act together and unanimously." Francis went on to challenge activists to "overcome distrust; promote a culture of solidarity, encounter, and dialogue; and be capable of showing responsibility for protecting the planet and the human family."

In all of his addresses, Francis uses simple, straightforward language, which allows his critics to claim he lacks the theological sophistication of his predecessors. The reality, however, is that Francis knows how his audience learns and he is speaking directly to them. Think of Jesus using parables to spread the Gospel message. And what even his critics can't deny is that Francis is a master with symbolism.

From washing the feet of a young Muslim woman on Holy Thursday to stopping to pray at a wall covered in graffiti calling for the liberation of the Palestinian people to using debris from shipwrecks carrying poor migrants as an altar, Francis knows that where he goes and what he does carries great weight. His actions are the message, so to speak. This also drove his January 2015 visit to Tacloban, a region in the Philippines where thousands had died fourteen months prior at the hands of one of the nation's worst typhoons. "When I saw in Rome that catastrophe, I felt I had to be here," he told the 200,000 people braving driving rain. "And on those very days, I decided to come here. I'm here to be with you." Environmental disasters could become more common because of climate change, and Francis doesn't want us to forget the human face of these storms.

Knowing that many climate change activists link global warming with a rise in powerful, deadly storms, Francis prepared a homily for the visit that once again called on Christians to take the earth's plight seriously. Though the homily was cut short by the weather, the Vatican released the prepared remarks, in which the pope said God calls on Christians to respect creation. "When we destroy our forests," he said, "ravage our soil and pollute our seas, we betray that noble calling." And while "using cleaner products or recycling what we use" are "important aspects," he said more must be done. "We need to see, with the eyes of faith, the beauty of God's saving plan, the link between the natural environment and the dignity of the human person."

Millions in the Philippines heard the pope's remarks during his visit, and on the way home, he had another message for those listening in. Asked who is to blame for the ecological crisis, he offered another sound bite perfect for the Twitter age: "It is man who continuously slaps nature in the face."

Pope Francis @Pontifex • 11 December 2014

Ecology is essential for the survival of mankind; it is a moral issue which affects all of us.

The debate over how to deal with a changing planet continues, but Francis's message is clear: something must be done. He's signed on to help protect the Amazon's water basin, and he minced no words when he said in March 2015, "humanity's future depends on our ability to care for [water] and protect it." The next month, the Vatican hosted a meeting with the head of the United Nations, Ban Ki-moon, to discuss ways forward on the issue. (In a sign that the world is far from united on the issue, a group of American climate change deniers held a rival meeting in Rome the day before.)

During a February 2015 morning Mass at Casa Santa Marta, Francis drew a line in the sand. Responding to critics who say that anyone who cares about the environment is some sort of green zealot, the pope said no, that they are simply Christian. "A Christian who does not protect creation, who does not let it grow, is a Christian who does not care about the work of God, that work that was born from the love of God for us," he said. "And this is the first response to the first creation: protect creation, make it grow."

Over the next several months, Francis would again repeat his calls for greater protection of the environment, culminating with *Laudato Si'* and its accompanying Twitterbomb. The pope's advisers said that clues to the encyclical were to be found in the pope's talks and Tweets over the previous several months. From his first days on Twitter through the latest Tweets highlighting the encyclical, Francis cannot be more clear that protecting the environment is a Christian virtue. There are some Christians who believe protecting the earth isn't a priority, especially if the true reward is in heaven. Others doubt that human beings contribute much to a suffering planet. Francis dismisses both these ideas, and he ties the care for creation to the care for the most marginalized. The pope, relating best to everyday people, even offered some practical ideas in his encyclical on how we could all contribute, "such as avoiding the use of plastic and paper, reducing water consumption, separating refuse, cooking only what can reasonably be consumed, showing care for other living beings, using public transport or carpooling, planting trees, turning off unnecessary lights, or any number of other practices." From the most powerful lawmakers and lobbyists to the everyday Catholic in the pew, Francis reminds us we all have a part to play.

 Pope Francis @Pontifex • 18 June 2015

What kind of world do we want to leave to those who come after us, to children who are now growing up?

 Pope Francis @Pontifex • 18 June 2015

The teachings of the Gospel have direct consequences for our way of thinking, feeling and living. #LaudatoSi

Pope Francis @Pontifex • 18 June 2015

Reducing greenhouse gasses requires honesty, courage and responsibility. #LaudatoSi

Pope Francis @Pontifex • 14 November 2013

Take care of God's creation. But above all, take care of people in need.

8

Pro-Life

WITH TRUMPETS BLARING AND FLAGS WAVING—BOTH THE yellow and gold of the Holy See and the blue and white of Argentina—Pope Francis entered Saint Peter's Square on March 19, 2013, about thirty minutes before his inaugural Mass as the Bishop of Rome. But before he reached the basilica, where he descended to pray in front of the tomb of Saint Peter, two seemingly unremarkable, yet quite telling, things happened. First, he blessed a baby someone handed him, and then he stopped the Popemobile so that he could greet a severely disabled man. Though it was impossible to know at the time, those two actions perfectly exemplify how Francis hopes Catholics approach life issues: broadly and personally. They also help give a human face to his Tweets about life.

In the first few months of his papacy, Francis steered clear of the abortion controversy. Catholics who protest abortion laws noticed. Francis presided over a Mass in June 2013 set aside to commemorate "Evangelium Vitae," or the Gospel of Life, planned during the reign of his predecessor, Pope Benedict XVI. Francis again didn't explicitly mention abortion, much to the alarm of organizers and attendees. This omission continued for several weeks, until a reporter forced the pope to confront the Church's central life issue.

The next month, activists in Brazil were disappointed that Francis hadn't challenged that country's push to liberalize abortion laws during his visit for World Youth Day. On his flight home from Rio, Francis was asked about this omission. "The Church has already expressed itself perfectly on that," he said. Anti-abortion advocates were stunned. Yet, had they looked at the pope's Twitter feed, they need not have worried. On May 13, weeks before the June Mass and his trip to Rio, Francis made his views quite clear, Tweeting:

 Pope Francis @Pontifex • 15 May 2013
It is God who gives life. Let us respect and love human life, especially vulnerable life in a mother's womb.

But a quick glance at the pope's Tweets reveals that Francis is trying to expand what it means to be pro-life. When Francis Tweets about life, he isn't trying to change centuries of Church teaching. Instead, he's lifting up pro-life teachings that have gotten lost in the conversation over abortion and marriage in recent decades. The Catholic Church is one of the fiercest advocates for life, and Francis wants to ensure that his followers understand this means widening our vision beyond a couple of hot-button topics. The pope's priorities are made clear on Twitter, directly to this virtual flock, without the noise and spin of others promoting their own agenda. When it comes to life, Francis is clear: the Church must fight for life at every age.

 Pope Francis @Pontifex • 6 May 2014

A society which abandons children and the elderly severs its roots and darkens its future.

 Pope Francis @Pontifex • 11 January 2014

No elderly person should be like an "exile" in our families. The elderly are a treasure for our society.

 Pope Francis @Pontifex • 25 October 2013

The "throw-away" culture produces many bitter fruits, from wasting food to isolating many elderly people.

Pope Francis @Pontifex • 26 April 2013

Dear young people, do not bury your talents, the gifts that God has given you! Do not be afraid to dream of great things!

Francis acknowledged in September 2013 that he was aware some in the Church were displeased with him because of the issue. "We cannot insist only on issues related to abortion, gay marriage, and the use of contraceptive methods. This is not possible. I have not spoken much about these things, and I was reprimanded for that," he told the Jesuit journals. Church teaching, he said, "is clear and I am a son of the Church, but it is not necessary to talk about these issues all the time." He went on, "the Church cannot be obsessed" with these few issues. It is up to Church leaders "to find a new balance; otherwise even the moral edifice of the Church is to fall like a house of cards, losing the freshness and fragrance of the Gospel." For Francis, following the "freshness and fragrance of the Gospel" means advocating for life at every stage, which he does regularly on Twitter.

Francis of Assisi, the pope's namesake, is said to have first spoken the line that one must preach the Gospel at all times and use words only when necessary. The now famous images of Pope Francis embracing babies, the elderly, the disfigured, and the disabled convey his concern for life, all life. His actions—and Tweets—challenge what has emerged as two distinct

Catholic tribes: the "pro-life Catholics," concerned primarily with abortion, contraception, and marriage; and "social justice Catholics," focused on poverty, the death penalty, and the economy. For Francis, no such distinction exists. Catholics are called on to vigorously defend all life, and he's showing how it's done.

To clear up any confusion, however, Francis delivered his most forceful remarks against abortion the day after the Jesuit interview was published, reiterating his call to protect all life but zeroing in on abortion, too. Speaking to a group of Catholic doctors, Francis laid out his beliefs about life. "In all its phases and at every age," he said, "human life is always sacred and always quality." Francis went on to lament what he termed a "'throwaway culture,' which has enslaved the hearts and minds of so many," a worldview that, according to Francis, "calls for the elimination of human beings, above all if they are physically or socially weaker." The Christian response to this, Francis said, must be "a decisive and unhesitating 'yes' to life."

Then, if any ambiguity remained about his stance on abortion, Francis cleared it up with one line: "Every unborn child, though unjustly condemned to be aborted, has the face of the Lord, who even before his birth, and then as soon as he was born, experienced the rejection of the world."

But again, he zoomed out, getting back to his insistence that Catholics care for all life. "And every old person," he said, "even if infirm and at the end of his days, carries with him the face of Christ. They must not be thrown away!"

That, in a nutshell, is Francis's position on life: all lives are sacred from conception to natural end. That has been the view of the Church for centuries. But Francis reminds Catholics—in word and deed—to emphasize the latter part of this teaching just as vigorously as the former.

For Francis, the "Gospel of Life" extends beyond the abortion wars, which are particularly venomous in the United States. His homily from the June Mass for life neatly sums up his thinking on the issue. People say no to life, he said, because of ideologies that exalt "selfishness, self-interest, profit, power, and pleasure," rather than love and concern "for the good of others." He Tweeted this message in June 2013:

 Pope Francis @Pontifex • 9 June 2013
With the "culture of waste", human life is no longer considered the primary value to be respected and protected.

A few months later, in a message to Catholics in England and Wales, he again upheld the need to protect all life, "even the weakest and most vulnerable, the sick, the old, the unborn and the poor." Francis wants Christians and others of good will to see the vulnerable as "masterpieces of God's creation, made in his own image, destined to live forever, and deserving of the utmost reverence and respect." This includes the unborn, the young, the old, and everyone in between.

Francis linked his opposition to abortion with a wider range of life issues most explicitly in *Evangelii Gaudium (The Joy of the Gospel),* his November 2013 apostolic exhortation—or letter to Catholics—that in many ways has become a blueprint for how he leads the Church. The defense of unborn life, he wrote, "is closely linked to the defense of each and every other human right. It involves the conviction that a human being is always sacred and inviolable, in any situation and at every stage of development. Human beings are ends in themselves and never a means of resolving other problems. Once this conviction disappears, so do solid and lasting foundations for the defense of human rights." For Francis, life is life, deserving of equal protection and zealous safeguarding at every stage.

Of particular concern to Francis are the elderly. The pope is acutely aware of the challenges the aged face, not least of which is their diminished role in society. Of no use to a culture that reveres money and youth over everything else, the elderly are often swept aside and not cared for in their final days. "We live in a time when the elderly do not count. It's awful to say, but they are discarded," he said, starkly, during a morning Mass in November 2013. But, he warned, it is the young who will ultimately suffer if they fail to see that in the elderly, "like a good vintage wine," lies much-needed wisdom and faith. "A people that does not care for its grandparents, a people that does not respect their grandparents," he said, "does not have a future, because they do not have a memory, they have lost their memory."

> Pope Francis @Pontifex • 17 June 2014
> **Sometimes we cast the elderly aside, but they are a precious treasure: to cast them aside is an injustice and an irreparable loss.**

Later on, while speaking to a group of palliative care specialists in March 2015, Francis again voiced his concern that the elderly weren't being treated with the respect they deserve. "Abandonment is the most serious 'illness' of the elderly and also the greatest injustice they can suffer," he said. "Those who have helped us grow must not be abandoned when they need our help, our love, and our tenderness." In other words, God loves all people, even if the world has no use for some. He said, "When life becomes very fragile and the end of earthly existence approaches, we feel the responsibility to assist and accompany the person in the best way." Or at least we should.

Like the elderly, who provide a powerful witness to many of life's challenges, the disabled are also hugely important pillars of Francis's pro-life vision. He's demonstrated this time and again, just like he did right before that first papal Mass. During a summer 2014 visit to the southern Italian region of Calabria, Francis asked his driver to pull over. Signs had been placed along the road asking Francis to stop to visit "an angel who has been waiting for you." So he did. Francis greeted and kissed the young woman, Roberta, who was lying on a stretcher. Local children and family members were stunned and visibly moved.

 Pope Francis @Pontifex • 14 July 2013

For a Christian, life is not the product of mere chance, but the fruit of a call and personal love.

There are the many iconic images of the pope greeting disabled and disfigured pilgrims in Saint Peter's Square. In follow-up interviews, families of those the pope blesses speak of how moving the experience was for them. Francis took this love for the disabled to another level in 2014. As we will read in the chapter on service, Francis celebrated Holy Thursday Mass, in which priests (and popes) commemorate Jesus washing the feet of his disciples, in a home for the elderly and disabled. There, Francis washed and kissed the disfigured and swollen feet of twelve residents, many seated in wheelchairs. Here was the powerful leader of one billion Catholics bowing down before those that society had cast aside. It was an example Francis wants his followers to emulate.

In addition to his acts of corporeal mercy, Francis has made it a priority to demonstrate a similar culture of encounter to the digital world as well. In February 2015, Francis participated in a Google Hangout with disabled kids from around the globe. His message for them was simple and powerful: share your insights with the rest of us. He told them that they possess a treasure chest, and that the world needs to learn what's inside. "If we keep it inside, it stays there inside," he said. "When we share it with others, the treasure multiplies itself, for that treasure is for others."

Similarly, in an address to groups of blind and deaf believers at the Vatican in March 2014, Francis noted that in the Gospels Jesus had a particular affinity for "those people marked by illness and disability." Today, the disabled help demonstrate what a culture of encounter looks like in practice. A disabled person, Francis said, "starting from his fragility, from his limitations," can show others how to encounter Jesus, one another, and the community. "In fact," he said, "only those who recognize their own fragility and their own limitations can build fraternal relations and solidarity, in the Church and society."

Francis, the pope of the periphery, gives voice to those who live on society's margins, the only place where "reality is understood," as he put it in a January 2014 talk at the Vatican. And yet he gives voice to this periphery on one of the largest social media platforms in the world, celebrating their innate talents and spiritual gifts to his 20 million followers. While Francis opposes abortion, he also fears that other lives are at risk, languishing on the edge, people who are in need of attention—the elderly, the sick, and even murderers condemned to die. These, as his everyday acts of mercy and Tweets tell us, are the lives he feels he must hold up, begging the world not to forget them or sweep them away.

Pope Francis @Pontifex • 22 January 2015
Every Life is a Gift. #marchforlife

When Francis Tweets about life, there's a dual purpose. On the one hand, the pope is encouraging those fighting for the Church's premiere life cause. But he's also reminding his followers not to forget about each and every life. This is the genius of Francis, not altering the content of Church teaching, but challenging Catholics to apply it in radically new ways.

Pope Francis @Pontifex • 7 February 2014
What zest life acquires when we allow ourselves to be filled by the love of God!

Pope Francis @Pontifex • 27 March 2015
Life is a precious gift, but we realize this only when we give it to others.

Speaking up for life, all life, is one of this vibrant pope's primary goals. After all, life is certainly an adventure worth living and sharing with others.

9

Sports

POPE FRANCIS, AN AVID SOCCER FAN SINCE BOYHOOD, TOOK TO Twitter at the start of the 2014 World Cup to "wish everyone a wonderful World Cup." He convinced millions watching around the world to "Pause for Prayer" before the start of the first game, in no small part because of his reach on Twitter. And by the end of the thirty-two days of play, Francis's beloved Argentines would play at least a couple of matches that gave Vatican watchers something to smile about. Sports, again, is one of those topics that the pope doesn't Tweet about too regularly, but when he does, it's because he has something to offer about the way we live our lives.

Pope Francis @Pontifex • 12 June 2014

I wish everyone a wonderful World Cup, played in a spirit of true fraternity.

On July 1 in Sao Paolo, Argentina faced Switzerland. In Rome, that meant the pope and his Swiss Guards would be on opposite sides. Francis even joked to some members of his protective service, "It's going to be war!" But they didn't mind. His army invited him to their barracks to watch the game on their big-screen TV. People joked: Would he be safe in their hands should Argentina prevail? The Vatican Communications office Tweeted a cartoon the day of the match, showing two jubilant Swiss Guards in front of a television, waving Swiss flags, cheering, and enjoying a couple of cold ones. In the corner, a miffed Pope Francis wallows. The cartoon, however, ended up being inaccurate. The Argentines defeated the Swiss 1–0 in the knockout round. The pope remained in good hands nonetheless.

Argentina continued to play well and earned a spot in the championship game, where they squared off against Germany, Pope Emeritus Benedict XVI's homeland. How would the rival popes react? Would they place a friendly wager? They would at least watch the game together, right? Social media had some fun with this. One image making the rounds superimposed the two popes' faces on members of their respective teams. Another showed the two popes praying side by side, with their nations' flags in thought bubbles over their heads. The caption: "May the best prayer win." (Though recognizing his new role as universal pastor, Francis actually promised not to offer up any prayers on Argentina's behalf.) Sadly, the anticipation of a papal showdown was not to be.

Rev. Federico Lombardi, the Vatican's spokesman who had bemusedly answered questions about soccer for weeks, said that Pope Benedict wasn't much of a soccer fan. Francis is, of course, but given that the game didn't start until late in the evening Rome time, it was unlikely that he'd be watching at all. It was probably for the best, as Argentina lost 1–0. This didn't stop the pope from Tweeting out a congratulatory message, praising the tournament for promoting its "culture of encounter."

 Pope Francis @Pontifex • 12 July 2014

The World Cup allowed people from different countries and religions to come together. May sport always promote the culture of encounter.

There are a number of strategies available to leaders who seek to change the world. One is to set the agenda and convince everyone that this is what we should be most focused on. Another strategy is to take what people are already doing and encourage and model for everyone a new framework for how to see it. With his Tweets regarding the World Cup and other sports, the Pope utilizes the latter strategy. In all his sports-related messages, he celebrates these occasions of leisure and enjoyment, but he also tries to remind us how best to approach these aspects of our lives. Guided by his Jesuit training, Francis sees value in sports not because they are overtly prayerful or holy, but because they are part of our lives. Everything we do, including leisure activities, should be able to be viewed as something sacred. Sports are no exception.

The Tweet above hinted at what Francis sees as the value that sports can have on faith, society, and children: to "promote the culture of encounter." In his first year as pope, Francis gave three major talks about sports: one to the members of the European Olympic Committees, another to athletes in the Paralympic Games, and a third on the anniversary of the foundation of the Italian Sports Center.

Speaking to the European Olympic Committees in November 2013, Pope Francis summed up his views on sports succinctly: They help form the human person and bring people together across all sorts of artificial boundaries. The Church, he said, "sees in sports a powerful instrument for the integral growth of the human person. Engaging in sports, in fact, rouses us to go beyond ourselves and our own self-interests in a healthy way." Francis highlighted the power of sports to permeate seemingly impenetrable borders. "The language of sports is universal," he said. "It extends across borders, language, race, religion and ideology; it possesses the capacity to unite people, together, by fostering dialogue and acceptance." Fans might see sports primarily as a diversion from real life. But

Francis reminds us that even in diversions, there are valuable lessons to be learned.

The pope's fascination with sports began when he was a boy, a fan of the San Lorenzo football club in Buenos Aires. The club enjoyed a spike in popularity following Francis's election, and its Catholic roots make the pope's connection all the more fitting.

In the early 1900s, a priest, Lorenzo Massa, allowed local boys to use Church property for a soccer field, rather than the unsafe street corner, on the condition that they make it to Mass on Sundays. The team that grew from this band of amateurs was eventually named after the priest, San Lorenzo de Almagro, and Pope Francis grew up near the stadium where they now play. He became a member in 2008: ID number 88235.

San Lorenzo won the Argentine soccer championship in 2013, and that December they traveled to Rome. In the middle of Saint Peter's Square, Francis held up the trophy for all to see. The team gave the pope a jersey— with "Francisco Campeon" ("Francis Champion") written on the back. With a big smile, Francis accepted the jersey and the trophy, both of which remain in Rome. In return, he gave the players an image of the Virgin Mary; they promised to keep it in the stadium.

Earlier that year, in August, the pope welcomed other big-name soccer stars to the Vatican. The national teams of Argentina and Italy were to play an exhibition match in the pope's honor, and they stopped by Saint Peter's to greet Francis. On hand was Argentine great

Lionel Messi, who smiled enthusiastically as he shook the pope's hand. The event turned out to be more than a pep rally. Francis reminded the athletes that, "for better or worse," they are role models in society and should take that seriously. "Dear players," he said, "you are very popular. People follow you, and not just on the field, but also off it. That's a social responsibility." And there was some symbolism packed into the event, too. While the pope received all the players publicly, only one got one-on-one time with Francis: Mario Balotelli.

Balotelli is something of a bad boy in the soccer world, his off-field antics, such as car crashes and setting off fireworks in his house, getting him in trouble. He's also black, and some soccer fans are known to hurl nasty insults toward players of different races and nationalities. Balotelli, of Ghanaian descent, has frequently been the subject of racist chants.

Given the pope's concern for the marginalized, it's easy to imagine why he might have chosen Balotelli for the private meeting. Balotelli, who turned just twenty-three the day before he met Francis, looked emotional following the private chat. As Francis has Tweeted, sports should promote peace and fraternity, not hate and division.

 Pope Francis @Pontifex • 25 July 2013

May sports always be a means of exchange and growth, never of violence and hate. #Rio2013 #JMJ

It's not only soccer with Pope Francis. (But let's be honest, it's mostly soccer. He is South American after all.) While the pope praised sports for bringing people together for mutual understanding, he had other virtues in mind when meeting with rugby players in November 2013. "Rugby is a very nice sport and I tell you I see it like that because it's tough, there's a lot of physical contact. But there's no violence, just great loyalty and respect," he said. "It's not a walk in the park and that's why I think it serves to build character and willpower."

As I write in the chapter on inequality, Francis is a harsh critic of libertarianism—the go-it-alone mentality infiltrating politics and society among young adults—and he sees in rugby an antidote to this ideology. "In rugby, you run toward the goal. This is a very beautiful word that makes us think about life. Because our entire life is in pursuit of a goal, and this quest is hard, requires struggle and commitment, but the important thing is not to run alone," he said. At just 40 characters, "The important thing is not to run alone," is a perfect Tweet to convey so much of what Francis teaches. He's the Tweetable pope because of what he publishes on Twitter, and because so much of what he says is ready for his followers to post themselves.

 Pope Francis @Pontifex • 31 January 2014
No one saves oneself. The community is essential.

Francis, born in 1936, is well beyond his physical prime, and he wasn't much of an athlete even when he was young. But that doesn't mean he can't see the value in sports for youth. In his address to the Italian Sports Center in June 2014, Francis called sports one of three key pillars for young people. "I find there are three paths for young people," he said, "the path of education, the path of sports and the path of work, when there are jobs for young people to start with!" (Francis never skips an opportunity to get a jab in at the lack of employment opportunities for the young.) He even suggested that, with solid education, sports, and work, "there wouldn't be dependencies: no drugs, no alcohol!" In the same talk, he extolled the teamwork required in many sports, exclaiming, "No individualism! No playing for yourselves!" He challenged young people to approach their faith like they do their sports, not settling for ties or "lukewarm lives, 'mediocre even-scored' lives: no, no! Go forward, seek victory always!" Francis concluded this talk as he has many others, by asking for prayers. "I ask you to pray for me, because I too play in my own game, which is your game, it is the game of the whole Church! Pray for me that I can play the game until the day the Lord calls me to himself." Again, sports aren't something ancillary to a life well lived. For Francis, sports offer an insight into the values that help us live meaningfully. That's why his Tweets about sports aren't just fun musings, but an invitation to see God in all things.

The game he talks about, presumably, is the life of a Christian, and not one of the actual games the Vatican hosts. You see, Francis has put his words into action, getting the Vatican into the sporting scene, too. Under Francis, the Vatican launched a cricket team, comprised of seminarians from places where cricket is popular. Reenacting the Protestant Reformation, the team even took on the Church of England's club in September 2014.

There's also the Clericus Cup, a soccer tournament for Catholic seminarians studying in Rome's pontifical colleges, held each year since 2007. And there was the Race of Faith in October 2013, for which a three-lane, hundred-meter track was laid down on the main thoroughfare entering Saint Peter's Square. Might we even see Olympic events held inside the Vatican walls in 2024? Maybe. Rome is making a bid, and the Vatican could play host to smaller events such as archery. Just don't expect to see Pope Francis there. "Best wishes also for Rome's bid to host the 2024 Olympic Games!" he said following a meeting with Italy's Olympic officials, but added, with a knowing smile given his advanced age, "I won't be around."

With just a handful of Tweets about sports, Pope Francis isn't exactly relying on soccer to remake the Church's image. But he uses his love of that game, and the popularity of other sports, to demonstrate that to be Catholic doesn't mean to turn away from the world. Instead, he urges his followers to see God even in the leisure activities we enjoy.

If the Church previously had been viewed in the popular culture for what it opposes, Francis wants to change the conversation. There's even something holy in rooting for your favorite team, he reminds us. It might take a few seconds to realize that, but his Tweets are perfectly suited to prompt that brief reflection. Then, back to the game. That's what this pope, and his Tweets, are all about: encouraging believers to consider how to make their own lives a bit more like Jesus's, even in seemingly nonsacred moments.

10

The Devil

AS WE'VE READ, FRANCIS IS A THOROUGHLY MODERN POPE, A breath of fresh air, happily meeting people where they are and encouraging Catholics not to hunker down, but to get out there, make a mess of things. One doesn't become the most influential world leader on Twitter by being out of touch with the modern world. But if there's one area where this pope is decidedly old-school, it's in the realm of how he talks about the reality of evil, often personified in the devil.

Pope Francis @Pontifex • 30 September 2014

Division within a Christian community is a very grave sin; it is the work of the devil.

Pope Francis @Pontifex • 6 March 2014

Let us pray for Christians who are victims of persecution, so that they may know how to respond to evil with good.

Pope Francis @Pontifex • 25 October 2014

Jesus' Cross shows the full force of evil, but also the full power of God's mercy.

Consider this: In his two years as pope, Francis has Tweeted about the devil so often that he's had to ascribe different names in order to keep Satan and his different forms relevant within the Twittersphere. Some of Francis's favorite names for Satan—from his common titles to Francis's own creative nomenclature—include:

+ Satan
+ The Demon
+ The Seducer
+ The Tempter
+ The Great Dragon
+ The Ancient Serpent
+ The Prince of This World
+ The Darkness
+ The Enemy
+ The Evil One
+ The Father of Hate

+ The Father of Lies
+ The Father of War
+ The Accuser

The Great Dragon and the Ancient Serpent may sound like Harry Potter characters, but the devil is no laughing matter for Francis. He takes the Enemy very seriously, and he preaches about it constantly. That the pope's views on evil aren't reported as often as his more progressive views—on women, gays, and the divorced, for example—probably says more about the narrative the media has constructed than it reflects the wide portfolio of Francis's actual beliefs. For Francis, evil exists and Christians had better start fighting the devil off lest the world go straight to hell.

The pope bluntly expressed this belief in a June 2013 message to pilgrims gathered in Saint Peter's Square: "It is enough to open a newspaper," he said, "and we see that around us there is the presence of evil, the devil is at work." Talk about "the devil" is likely to conjure images of horns and hoofs, sulfur and shrieking. But for Francis, it's a touch more complicated. While not refusing to dismiss evil as an allegorical phenomenon, as many Western Christians are wont to do, the pope links evil and the devil to temptation as well as to personal choices and interactions. His upbringing in Latin America, coupled with his background as a Jesuit, informs his fixation on the devil. One thing is clear: Francis wants his followers to take the devil seriously.

Pope Francis @Pontifex • 10 September 2013

The only war that we must all fight is the one against evil #prayforpeace

Pope Francis @Pontifex • 8 October 2013

The secret of Christian living is love. Only love fills the empty spaces caused by evil.

Pope Francis @Pontifex • 1 November 2014

A good example brings about so much good, but hypocrisy brings about much evil.

Francis is self-aware, and he realizes that all his talk about the devil and evil can be a bit off-putting to modern sensibilities. He's acknowledged this a couple of times. In October 2013, for instance, during a morning Mass at his residence, Francis preached on the need for Christians to protect themselves from the devil's deceit. Anticipating the objections from those in the pews, Francis quoted his skeptics, saying, "But, Father, you are a little ancient. You are frightening us with these things." A few months later, in April, Francis preached again about the devil, warning Christians not to give in to temptation. Again anticipating objections from the congregation, he said, "But Father, how old-fashioned you are to speak about the devil in the twenty-first century."

In both instances, however, Francis rejected the claims that his ideas were too dusty for such a modern time. To those gathered in God's name in October, he said, "No, it is not me! It is the Gospel! And these are not lies, it is the word of the Lord!" he preached. In April, he issued a similar refrain: "Look, the devil is present. The devil is here, even in the twenty-first century! And we mustn't be naive, right? We must learn from the Gospel how to fight against Satan."

 Pope Francis @Pontifex • 18 October 2013

We cannot give up in the face of evil. God is Love and he has defeated evil through Christ's death and resurrection.

The question of evil has confounded theologians for centuries, but Francis wants to make one thing clear: evil and the devil exist. People invite evil into their hearts by giving in to temptation, often through envy and jealousy. In a January 2014 sermon during morning Mass, Francis said, "Jealousy leads to murder. Envy leads to murder. It was this door, the door of envy, through which the devil entered the world. Jealousy and envy open the doors to all evil things."

During a talk to a group of children on the outskirts of Rome in February 2015, Francis said that allowing this kind of evil to lurk in the heart leads to lies, hate, and war. It can rip apart families. "Parents," he told them, "suffer because their children do not speak to each other, or with the wife of a son. And so this jealousy and envy, it is sowed by the devil." According to Francis, evil is strong, but human beings must not let it into their lives, where it spreads, capable of tearing apart communities. It's a seemingly simple message, one suited for Twitter, but it also prompts deep reflection about our otherwise modern lives.

 Pope Francis @Pontifex • 2 November 2013

The fight against evil is long and difficult. It is essential to pray constantly and to be patient.

During an October 2014 Mass, Francis asked worshippers, "How often do wicked thoughts, wicked intentions, jealousy, envy enter in?" "So many things that enter in. But who has opened that door?" He said that, without proper precautions, the heart becomes "a piazza, where everything comes and goes." What's more, Christians and people of good will are especially susceptible to evil, the pope argued in May 2014, because "the devil cannot stand seeing the sanctity of a church or the sanctity of a person without trying to do something." Evil exists, the pope believes, but works because of Christion apathy.

Pope Francis @Pontifex • 30 September 2013

Where we find hate and darkness, may we bring love and hope, in order to give a more human face to society.

Francis worries that evil rips apart Christian communities, as evidenced by the Tweet he sent on September 30, but what about entire nations? In the spring of 2015 Francis found himself in a bit of hot water after a friend made public an e-mail in which the pope worried about the "Mexicanization" of his native Argentina. He explained that he meant no offense. He was simply saying that he worried Argentina's economic troubles might lead to a rise in drug gangs, not unlike those that continue to haunt Mexico and other Latin American nations today. Francis granted an interview to a Mexican journalist from Televisa to explain. He compared "Mexicanization" with "Balkanization," and noted that Mexico's political leaders had accepted his apology. But, he said, the violence plaguing Mexico was a serious concern. "I think that the devil punishes Mexico with a lot of problems," he said. More room for controversy, but Francis explained.

He noted Mexico's rich Catholic history, including the Virgin of Guadalupe and the Mexican martyrs of the early twentieth century. He said that because Mexico had been so blessed by religious fervor, "I

believe the devil is making Mexico pay, don't you?"
Some Mexican leaders were outraged, seeing in
the pope's words excuses for corrupt officials and
drug lords. (Of course, his frequent condemnation
of corruption and drugs eventually discounted this
theory.)

So if evil can tear apart lives, families, communities,
and even nations, is all lost to the devil? Of course not!
Francis is a Christian, and the central motif is the
triumph of good over evil, life over death. A few days
after his election, Francis offered Christians some
practical ways they can resist the temptation of the
Father of Lies.

 Pope Francis @Pontifex • 24 March 2013
**We must not believe the Evil One when
he tells us that there is nothing we can do
in the face of violence, injustice and sin.**

Like his fervent belief in evil itself, one of the pope's
solutions is also decidedly old-school. In a homily on
September 29, 2014, the Feast of the Archangels,
Francis reminded Christians that angels are allies
in the great cosmic battle. Angels exist and they are
present in order to help in our fight against evil! The
devil, he said, "presents things as if they were good, but
his intention is destruction. And the angels defend us!"
Angels, he explained, defend Jesus and his followers.
"This is why the Church honors the angels, because

they are the ones who will be in the glory of God, they are in the glory of God, because they defend the great hidden mystery of God—namely, that the Word was made flesh."

As he's Tweeted, Christians are called to struggle against evil. "The struggle is a daily reality in Christian life," he said, "in our hearts, in our lives, in our families, in our people, in our churches. If we do not struggle, we will be defeated." The struggle will be won with love.

 Pope Francis @Pontifex • 22 October 2013

The crucifix does not signify defeat or failure. It reveals to us the Love that overcomes evil and sin.

 Pope Francis @Pontifex • 31 March 2014

Lent is a time to change direction, to respond to the reality of evil and poverty.

 Pope Francis @Pontifex • 5 September 2013

There is no such thing as low-cost Christianity. Following Jesus means swimming against the tide, renouncing evil and selfishness.

Another way for Christians to protect themselves against evil and the devil, according to Francis, is through a daily examination of conscience. This is a traditional Catholic exercise often associated with the sacrament of reconciliation or confession, and one with a deep Jesuit connection. "Who of us, at night, at the end of the day, remains by himself, by herself, and asks the question: What happened today in my heart? What happened? What things passed through my heart?" he asked those gathered for Mass at Casa Santa Marta in October 2014. "We need to guard our hearts, where the Holy Spirit dwells, so that other spirits do not enter," he said, urging Christians "to guard the heart, as a house."

This kind of examination of conscience is profoundly Jesuit. Ignatian spirituality prompts individuals to engage in the examen, a daily reflection on one's thoughts and deeds, looking for the moments when God was near and when God was far. Over time, the theory goes, practitioners will be able to develop habits to ensure that they are open to God's will and follow it closely. The inverse is also true, as Francis has repeated. A daily examination of conscience can help individuals discern envy and jealously in their lives, hopefully leading to the realization that the problem needs addressing.

Since being elected Pope, Francis has Tweeted about the devil and evil close to twenty times, and his Tweets have been favorited and re-Tweeted tens of thousands of times. When the pope Tweets about evil, he's using a modern medium to spread an ancient belief, perhaps the best example of how Francis continues to make the old new. Though he has yet to change much about the Church's dogma, Francis has prompted the world to look at the Catholic Church in a new light. Whether his millions of Twitter followers will be persuaded by his arguments on the devil remains an open question, but he's certainly reinvigorated a conversation, one that's been going on for millennia.

The pope's Tweets about the Evil One are emblematic of all his Tweets. They're not just ideas or theological questions for us to ponder, though they do make us think. Rather, they are calls to action, in which Francis asks his followers to do something concrete.

In the case of the devil, Francis wants Christians to be vigilant against the mundane ways evil makes its way through the world. Do we do things in our own lives that make the world a bit less just, like gossiping, perhaps? Or, proactively, are there things we can do that invite goodness, rather than evil, to flourish? These are the things Francis turns our minds to and asks us to act on thereafter.

For Francis, using the ancient categories of devils, angels, and evil is never a way of diminishing human responsibility. It's just that we must be vigilant both in our souls and in our communities to fight against those vices and actions that allow evil an entry point. In fact, the primary playing field for the devil, according to Francis, is the human heart. It's only through a daily examination of our experiences with God and of our souls that we will be able to do the work God has called us to do: to love and serve others in a spirit of compassion and mercy. And there is nothing antiquated about that.

11

Inequality

AN UNEXPECTED TITLE SHOT UP TO THE TOP OF THE *NEW York Times* bestseller list in spring 2014, ultimately becoming the most successful book ever published by Harvard University Press. Translated from a relatively unknown French tome on economics, the English-language translation was making waves in the United States and around the world. The ideas contained in Thomas Piketty's *Capital in the Twenty-First Century* provided fresh fodder for social progressives concerned about the high rates of economic inequality not seen in the Western world in nearly a century.

During the media frenzy surrounding Piketty's book—it sold out on web giant Amazon—Pope Francis delivered perhaps his sharpest, and shortest, critique of social inequality, Tweeting:

Pope Francis @Pontifex • 28 April 2014
Inequality is the root of social evil.

Media buzzed. "Could it be that the Pope is weighing in on the fervor sparked by French economist Thomas Piketty's current bestseller, *Capital in the Twenty-First Century*?" asked the *Huffington Post*. *The Daily Beast* had the same thought: "Has Pope Francis been reading Thomas Piketty?" *Salon,* the lefty American web journal, took it a step further, gushing: "Your move, Piketty."

Did Pope Francis read Piketty's work? Maybe, but he certainly wasn't endorsing the book via Twitter. And, more tellingly, Pope Francis had been warning about social inequality well before Piketty's book arrived on the scene. Consider this: In November 2013, just months after the pope's election, and months before Piketty's book made a splash, *New York* magazine published a tongue-in-cheek online quiz by Dan Amira entitled "Bill de Blasio or the Pope?" Readers were asked to decipher whether comments on social inequality were made by the head of the Catholic Church, or the ultra-progressive mayor of New York City, who is known for railing against the extreme stratification there. Here, you try:

Some people continue to defend trickle-down theories which assume that economic growth, encouraged by a free market, will inevitably succeed in bringing about greater justice and inclusiveness.

Is it the Democratic mayor of New York railing against Reaganomics, or the Argentine-born pontiff slamming libertarian economics? Correct answer: Pope Francis.

Give it another go:

Today everything comes under the laws of competition and the survival of the fittest, where the powerful feed upon the powerless.

An embattled politico throwing red meat to his liberal base, or the shepherd of more than one billion Catholics? Correct answer: Pope Francis, again.

Okay, one last try:

Money must serve, not rule!

It's Pope Francis, yet again!

The quiz was prompted by the publication of *Evangelii Gaudium* in November 2013, an apostolic letter from the pope to Catholics around the world that served as something of an early blueprint of his priorities as pope. Several sections are devoted to social inequality. (The quotes above all come from this document, released just eight months after the pope's election.) Francis has also Tweeted nuggets of wisdom from this document on a few occasions.

Pope Francis @Pontifex • 26 April 2014

None of us can think we are exempt from concern for the poor and for social justice (EG 201).

Pope Francis's views on the economy and social inequality don't rely exclusively on textbooks and theories. Instead, they are derived from his experience of working and living alongside the poor in Buenos Aires, where he served as archbishop. In his interview with Jesuit magazines, Francis put it like this: "When it comes to social issues, it is one thing to have a meeting to study the problem of drugs in a slum neighborhood and quite another thing to go there, live there and understand the problem from the inside and study it."

Pope Francis @Pontifex • 24 July 2014

When one lives attached to money, pride or power, it is impossible to be truly happy.

Pope Francis @Pontifex • 29 October 2013

If money and material things become the center of our lives, they seize us and make us slaves.

Pope Francis @Pontifex • 25 July 2013

The measure of the greatness of a society is found in the way it treats those most in need, those who have nothing apart from their poverty.

Pope Francis spent a great deal of time in Buenos Aires slums, ministering to the poorest. Drug addiction ran rampant there, especially among those whose lives seemed useless to those in the profit-making world: the sick, the unemployed, and even young adults. He saw firsthand how inequality so often leads to suffering, addiction, and sometimes death.

During his visit to Brazil for World Youth Day in 2013, Francis made a special point to visit a favela, or slum, and offered hope to those who lived there. "To you and all," he said, "I repeat: never yield to discouragement, do not lose trust, do not allow your hope to be extinguished. Situations can change, people can change." The pope ties the personal to the societal. For Francis, being with the poor isn't just about serving them, but learning from them. Standing shoulder to shoulder with someone unable to find work to provide for his family, who succumbs to drugs to ease the pain, is a much better argument for equality than any textbook.

"No amount of peace-building will be able to last," he said, "nor will harmony and happiness be attained in a society that ignores, pushes to the margins or excludes a part of itself."

Condemning social inequality takes up quite a bit of *Evangelii Gaudium*. "Just as the commandment 'Thou shalt not kill' sets a clear limit in order to safeguard the value of human life, today we also have to say 'thou shalt not' to an economy of exclusion and inequality. Such an economy kills," the pope writes there.

Again, this is a guy who's great with quips, getting deep messages across with just a few words, many times in memorable sound bites well below Twitter's 140 character maximum. He continues in *Evangelii Gaudium*, "How can it be that it is not a news item when an elderly homeless person dies of exposure, but it is news when the stock market loses two points? This is a case of exclusion." He's taken this same argument to Twitter.

 Pope Francis @Pontifex • 19 December 2013

Let us pray that God grant us the grace of knowing a world where no one dies of hunger.

Francis believes entire economies are increasingly geared toward serving the rich while discarding the poor, and governments seem to play along. Many in power often say that money for security must trump money for social programs. When government money is tight, as it is almost everywhere, the military still gets what it wants while social welfare programs are reduced or eliminated. Pope Francis calls out this paradox, noting that the resulting social inequality is a security threat in itself, leading to the kind of violence defense spending hopes to eliminate. "Inequality eventually engenders a violence which recourse to arms cannot and never will be able to resolve," he writes in *Evangelii Gaudium*. "It serves only to offer false hopes to those clamoring for heightened security, even though nowadays we know that weapons and violence, rather than providing solutions, create new and more serious conflicts."

 Pope Francis @Pontifex • 26 October 2013

Too often we participate in the globalization of indifference. May we strive instead to live global solidarity.

 Pope Francis @Pontifex • 12 June 2013

How many kinds of moral and material poverty we face today as a result of denying God and putting so many idols in his place!

A pope from Latin America means a pope who has seen it all when it comes to economics: the seemingly limitless power of capitalism to the north, the allure of radical forms of socialism, and the effect of inequality on the poor. His work as a Jesuit means he's spent time on the peripheries, with the poor, and has reflected on what they can teach the Church. But as pope, he's subject to some blowback, especially from some conservative provocateurs who took it for granted that the Catholic hierarchy was always on their side. (Which has never been the case, by the way, even with the last two popes, who were often labeled conservatives theologically, but who were quite progressive regarding their critiques of consumer capitalism.)

In the days following the pope's apostolic exhortation, the right-wing American radio personality Rush Limbaugh blasted Pope Francis. He said he had admired the pope but suspected he was playing to the liberal media. "But this," he said, referring to *Evangelii Gaudium,* was too much. "The pope has gone beyond Catholicism here. This is pure political. This is pure Marxism coming out of the mouth of the pope." Other critics were a touch more thoughtful, but shared the $300-million-net-worth Limbaugh's sentiments. Samuel Gregg, who works for the libertarian-leaning Acton Institute, questioned the pope's ability to offer thoughts on economic systems. He wrote, "a number of claims made by this document and some of the assumptions underlying those statements are rather questionable." Others simply said the pope should stick to religion, not economics.

The reality, of course, is that Pope Francis is hardly deviating from recent Catholic teaching on the economy. His predecessor, Pope Benedict XVI, who appealed to conservative Catholics because of his support for traditional liturgy and emphasis on life and marriage issues, was perhaps to the left of Francis on economic issues. Under Pope Benedict, the Vatican released a document in 2011 calling for something of a new world order, a "shared body of rules to manage the global financial market." But back to Francis: Did he cower in the face of all this criticism? Nah.

In a December 2013 interview with the Italian newspaper *La Stampa,* the pope defended his ideas, and even gently teased his critics. It's difficult not to see Francis giving a sly smile and subtle wink when he said, "The Marxist ideology is wrong. But I have met many Marxists in my life who are good people, so I don't feel offended." Rather than retreat, he dug in, sticking by his argument that the current situation harms the poor. "The promise was that when the glass was full, it would overflow, benefitting the poor. But what happens instead is that when the glass is full, it magically gets bigger, nothing ever comes out for the poor," he said. "I was not, I repeat, speaking from a technical point of view but according to the Church's social doctrine. This does not mean being a Marxist."

The thing about Pope Francis is that his words are meant to challenge not just the powerful and connected, but all believers. I'll admit that more than once, when rushing past a homeless person asking for change en route to a meeting or to see friends for dinner, I've had pangs of guilt. Should I have stopped and given a dollar or two? I always try to smile and acknowledge the person, but could I do more? The pope's answer appears to be yes.

> **Pope Francis** @Pontifex • 7 June 2013
> **Consumerism has accustomed us to waste. But throwing food away is like stealing it from the poor and hungry.**

> **Pope Francis** @Pontifex • 9 December 2013
> **If we see someone who needs help, do we stop? There is so much suffering and poverty, and a great need for good Samaritans.**

> **Pope Francis** @Pontifex • 12 March 2015
> **Beware of getting too comfortable! When we are comfortable, it's easy to forget other people.**

> **Pope Francis** @Pontifex • 5 August 2014
> **If you hoard material possessions, they will rob you of your soul.**

During a speech welcoming several papal ambassadors in May 2013, Francis challenged those present, and indeed the whole Catholic world, to consider the words of Saint John Chrysostom: "Not to share your goods with the poor is to rob them and deprive them of life."

Some wealthy Catholics have complained that Pope Francis talks too much about the poor, that he doesn't spend enough time addressing the concerns of the rest of his flock. They ask, Why should we keep donating to renovate churches and finance charities if the pope is so hostile to money? Francis agrees that he spends more time catering to the poor. During the same speech, he said, "The pope loves everyone, rich and poor alike, but the pope has the duty, in Christ's name, to remind the rich to help the poor, to respect them, to promote them."

There you have it. If you feel that Pope Francis talks, and Tweets, about the poor a lot, and the economic systems that keep them that way, resulting in unprecedented levels of inequality, you're right. He knows it, too. So the next time Pope Francis Tweets about inequality, remember: He doesn't care if you think he's a Marxist, if you question his intellectual ability, or if you think he's not speaking enough to the middle and upper classes. He's speaking from a long tradition of Catholic teaching, that stretches back to Jesus, about the need to make sure no one is left behind. Only, unlike his predecessors in the Vatican, he's doing it 140 characters at a time.

12

Work

Long before he was elevated to Bishop of Rome, Pope Francis held a string of odd jobs as a young man in Buenos Aires. He swept floors as a teenager. Later, he ran tests in chemistry labs. He once worked as a bouncer. No turning the other cheek there. Later on, he taught students literature and psychology. Like many people, Francis started his career with low-skilled work and eventually climbed up the ladder, finding a passion, and along with it, dignity and hope. Perhaps that's why work—and the financial, mental, and even spiritual benefits that accompany it—has emerged as one of the pope's primary issues in his speeches and homilies, as well as on Twitter.

When Pope Francis Tweets about work, he has two things in mind. First, as he so often does in his homilies, speeches, and prepared statements, he uses his Tweets to advocate for decent employment opportunities for everyone, extolling the many benefits of solid work.

Pope Francis @Pontifex • 24 June 2014

How I wish everyone had decent work! It is essential for human dignity.

Pope Francis @Pontifex • 7 May 2015

When we cannot earn our own bread, we lose our dignity. This is a tragedy today, especially for the young.

Pope Francis @Pontifex • 11 November 2014

Work is so important for human dignity, for building up a family, for peace!

Second, like he does with prayer and life, he wants to make sure his followers aren't separating faith from other parts of their lives. He urges his followers not to check their beliefs at the office door. This doesn't mean proselytizing, but living out Christian values, at all times, even in the workplace. Francis is taking more than a century of Catholic teaching on the rights of workers and placing it neatly on a rather modern platform, Tweeting out his support for the rights of everyone to decent employment. Taking a look at some of the pope's speeches and homily about the dignity of work helps to flesh out his Tweets a bit more and equips us to understand better why work is so important to this pope.

 Pope Francis @Pontifex • 30 May 2014

Every Christian can witness to God in the workplace, not only with words, but above all with an honest life.

 Pope Francis @Pontifex • 23 May 2013

Do I take the Gospel message of reconciliation and love into the places where I live and work?

Pope Francis @Pontifex • 16 May 2013

We cannot be part-time Christians! We should seek to live our faith at every moment of every day.

Much of the world devotes May 1 to holding up the rights of workers, known as the International Day of the Worker, or May Day. In 1955, hoping to place a Christian patina on this thoroughly secular celebration of the worker, Pope Pius XII dubbed the first of May the Feast of Saint Joseph the Worker, a day for Catholic leaders to speak up for the rights of workers. The modern Catholic labor movement began in 1891 with Pope Leo XIII's seminal encyclical *Rerum Novarum,* and in his 2013 Saint Joseph Day address, Pope Francis added another powerful papal voice to this long Catholic tradition.

That day, Francis began his morning, as he often does, with Mass. He often invites Vatican workers—gardeners, cooks, cleaners—to join him, along with bishops, priests, and nuns. A few days earlier and a world away in Dhaka, Bangladesh, a garment factory had collapsed, claiming the lives of more than a thousand workers. Their pay was just fifty dollars each month; they toiled for hours in unsafe and uncomfortable conditions. More than half the dead were women, and many of their children perished in the accident as well. Reading about the accident in *L'Osservatore Romano,* the Vatican's newspaper, Francis was outraged. Bodies were still being pulled from the wreckages as protesters marched through Bangladesh. Francis symbolically joined them during his morning homily.

"This is called slave labor!" Francis exclaimed. "Not paying fairly, not giving a job because you are only looking at balance sheets, only looking at how to make a profit. That goes against God!" Many of the garments being created in Bangladesh were for wealthier people far away from the poor neighborhoods where the workers lived. Recounting a story told by a medieval rabbi about the Tower of Babel, in which workers left to die were met with a shrug but fallen bricks were mourned over, Francis lamented that not much had changed. "People are less important than things that make a profit for those who have political, social, and economic power," he said.

Later that day, Francis read a message on work during his general weekly audience to the pilgrims gathered below in Saint Peter's Square. Reflecting on the Gospel passage for the day from Matthew, Francis remarked that Jesus lived a human life, learning carpentry from his father, Joseph, whose feast day was being celebrated. Jesus worked, the pope reminded those gathered, a fact that "reminds us of the dignity and importance of work."

Connecting work to his concern for the environment and the poor, Francis said that in Genesis, God calls on human beings to nurture and protect the earth, "caring for it through their work." Work, he said, is part of God's plan for human beings, a way for people to "share in the work of creation!" The pope took it a step further, boldly stating, "Work is fundamental to the dignity of a person." Work, he said, "gives one the ability to maintain oneself, one's family, to contribute to the growth of one's own nation."

This message was delivered just a few months into his pontificate, but Francis had already become something of a sensation on the political left, because of his emphasis on the poor and the environment. But his May Day message about the dignity of work struck a chord with more conservative circles, those who believe that government welfare programs perpetuate poverty and do little to promote dignity. Did they have an ally in Francis after all? Conservative blogs in the United States excerpted this speech with abandon, and they were right: Francis clearly sees productive work as a component to a fulfilling life. But, as Pope Francis Tweeted the next day, there's more to the message.

 Pope Francis @Pontifex • 2 May 2013
My thoughts turn to all who are unemployed, often as a result of a self-centred mindset bent on profit at any cost.

For Francis, not having access to dignified work isn't the result of laziness, but of systems that place profits over people. "I am thinking of how many, and not only young people, are unemployed, often due to a purely economic conception of society, which places profit selfishly, beyond the parameters of social justice," he said in his May Day message. Even those who have jobs aren't immune from this kind of abuse, such as those who died in Bangladesh. "How many people worldwide are victims of this type of slavery," he asked, "when the person is at the service of his or her work, while work should offer a service to people so that they may have dignity?"

Dignity is a constant theme in so many of the pope's writings, homilies, and speeches, and his talk about work is no different. For Francis, food pantries and soup kitchens alone aren't enough—though in many situations they are certainly necessary. "The problem," he said during a July 2014 homily in Molise in southern Italy, "is not being able to bring bread to the table at home: this is a serious problem, this takes away our dignity." He said that hunger can be addressed, by visiting food pantries for example, but that the "most serious problem is that of dignity. For this reason we must work and defend the dignity that work gives us." Later that year, in an October address to a group of activists at the Vatican, Francis reiterated his message, stating, "there is no worse material poverty than one that does not allow for earning one's bread." He said that all workers must be granted "the right to fitting remuneration, to social security, and to retirement coverage."

Pope Francis @Pontifex • 11 June 2015

Where there is no work, there is no dignity.

But to achieve these things, Christians must dare to take initiative to try new things, as Francis said in a video prepared for the Festival of Catholic Social Teaching in Verona the following month. Though lamenting that governments often say there is no money to invest in the poor while furthering military programs and kickbacks for the rich, Francis said money alone can't solve all the economic problems facing the world. "We cannot ask money to do what only people can do or create. Money alone will not create development; to promote development we need people who have the courage to take the initiative," he said. "Taking the initiative means overcoming excessive aid."

Work is clearly important to Francis, but there's a dark side to employment that he finds especially troubling: exploitation and slave labor. As he noted following the factory collapse in Bangladesh, low wages are a form of slavery. Speaking to crowds in the southern Italian region of Scampìa in March 2015, Francis slammed what he termed "half jobs," arrangements that pay little and offer even fewer benefits. Using some of his strongest language about the issue, the pope lashed out at employers who take advantage of the poor, knowing full well that people will work for little because there are so few options. "This is slavery," he said, "this is exploitation. It is not human, it is not Christian. If someone doing this described himself as a Christian, he is a liar." Pope Francis is being radical here. He's stating quite boldly that those business owners who place profits over people aren't Christian. We all have a right to jobs, the pope is saying, and good jobs that keep us safe as well.

In Francis's crusade for better employment, the way women are treated—and mistreated—is of particular concern. Under the pope's leadership, the Vatican has become a major player in the global fight against human trafficking. In February 2015, Francis commemorated the first International Day of Prayer and Awareness Against Human Trafficking. In his weekly Angelus address, he offered a prayer for "the many men, women, and children who are enslaved, exploited, abused as instruments of labor or of pleasure, who are often tortured and mutilated." Women, in particular, suffer at the hands of traffickers, who promise jobs and better lives but so often trap them in sexual violence. Francis led the crowd in a recitation of a Hail Mary, and he called on governments to "remove the causes of this shameful wound . . . a wound that is unworthy of civil society."

A few months later, Francis again voiced his support for women, this time calling for equal pay in the workplace, a particularly neuralgic issue in the United States. In a discussion about the need for Christians to witness to the benefits of marriage, Francis said women and men must have equality in the workplace. "Equality enjoyed by the spouses must produce new fruit: equal opportunities in the workplace; a new valuing of motherhood and fatherhood; and a greater appreciation for the openness of families to those most in need," he said. He called those who blame greater rights for women outside the home for the decrease in the number of marriages "chauvinistic" and said it's a "Christian duty" to fight for equality in the workplace.

The lack of employment opportunities for young people is also especially troubling for Pope Francis. On his way to Rio in July 2013 to celebrate World Youth Day, he slammed companies and economic systems that see young people as "disposable." Citing youth unemployment reaching close to 50 percent in some European countries, he said society risked "having a generation that hasn't held a job," and repeated his exhortation that working provides dignity. "Young people are in a crisis," he said. He doubled down in an October 2013 interview with the Italian newspaper *La Repubblica,* calling loneliness among the elderly and unemployment among the youth two of the greatest challenges facing the world today. The problem of youth unemployment is so dangerous, Francis said, because without employment, it's difficult to imagine a future, and thus marriage is delayed and families put off.

Pope Francis @Pontifex • 14 October 2014

O Lord, comfort all those who suffer, especially the sick, the poor and the unemployed.

In his 2014 Lenten message, Francis went even further, linking youth unemployment to addiction, loneliness, and even suicide. Denouncing systems that create poverty, Francis explained that unemployment leads to destitution, "poverty without faith, without support, without hope." For young people this can be especially toxic. "When power, luxury, and money become idols, they take priority over the need for a fair distribution of wealth," which can lead to "slavery to vice and sin," such as "alcohol, drugs, gambling, or pornography." This, Francis warns, "can be considered impending suicide."

But Francis is a man of joy and hope, rooted in the Resurrection, and he believes this faith has the potential to transform even the most belligerent economic systems. While not one to shy away from pontificating about the many maladies affecting people throughout the world, he warns Christians not to lose sight of the possibility of transformation. Speaking to a group of Italian steelworkers in March 2014, Francis repeated his belief that work is essential in helping individuals "be fully realized" in their "intellectual, creative, and manual capacities." But rising and stubborn unemployment threatened this, "the consequence of an economic system that is no longer able to create work, because it has placed at its center the idol of money." But there is hope, he told the workers, because of creativity and the Gospel.

Addressing the unemployment crisis means using "tools of creativity and solidarity," he said. While the challenges are great, "do not let yourselves be trapped in the vortex of pessimism!" Rather, "if everyone does his part, if we all put the human person and his dignity at the center, and if we consolidate an attitude of solidarity and fraternal sharing, inspired by the Gospel, we can emerge from the swamp of this difficult and burdensome period of economic turmoil."

Christians are called to follow the teachings of Jesus in every area of our lives. Work is no exception, as Francis has made clear on Twitter. Titans of industry are called to share the wealth through stable, fruitful employment opportunities for others. Making sure not to lose sight of the basic Christian notion that people are more important than profits is essential. If we aren't in positions of power, Francis still has a message for us. Are we honest at work? Do we treat others with respect?

When Pope Francis Tweets and talks about poverty, as he often does, it's essential to remember that a key component to overcoming this "scandal" is work. And the larger picture is this: Greed had replaced God. One of the symptoms of this new reality is a lack of good jobs. Without them, Francis believes, the future is lost.

13

War

POPES OF LATE TEND TO BE ANTI-WAR, AN UNSURPRISING revelation given that they lead a religion founded upon the teachings of Jesus, a radical pacifist. Both Pope John Paul II and Pope Benedict XVI lived through the horror of World War II in Europe, shaping their staunchly anti-war views. But what about a pope from the New World?

The extent to which Pope Francis has been willing to lend his moral voice into debates about war and peace has been remarkable: shocking and infuriating to some, welcome and heartening to others. Though he's Tweeted explicitly about war just a dozen times or so, Francis's #PrayForPeace hashtag campaign has taken on a range of war-related causes. When he launched it in September 2013, the hashtag became a global phenomenon almost instantly. In just a couple of weeks, it was used more than 260,000 times, referenced on Twitter more than the pope himself. Today, #PrayForPeace has become the pope's go-to hashtag when Tweeting about global conflict.

Pope Francis @Pontifex • 10 August 2014

An appeal to all families: when you say your prayers, remember all those forced from their homes in Iraq. #PrayForPeace

Pope Francis @Pontifex • 8 June 2014

I ask all people of good will to join us today in praying for peace in the Middle East. #weprayforpeace

Pope Francis @Pontifex • 15 February 2014

Let us pray for peace in Africa, especially in the Central African Republic and in South Sudan. #prayforpeace

The story of how #PrayForPeace became a global sensation starts with Syria. People across the world were horrified by the use of chemical weapons against civilians in the midst of a bloody civil war in Syria during the summer months of 2013. The United States and other nations were considering a bombing campaign to try to halt some of the carnage. The case for war was compelling: How could people sit around and do nothing while innocents suffered and died at the hands of a ruthless dictator?

But Pope Francis led the resistance to the "peace through war" mantra. Aware that the "collateral damage" of bombs can be as bad as the atrocities they're meant to stop, he called on Catholics around the world instead to pray for peace in Syria. Channeling his predecessor, Pope Paul VI, who told the United Nations in 1965, "No more war, war never again," the pope Tweeted his intentions. He mobilized Catholics around the world, asking them, through Twitter, to pray, fast, and protest.

Pope Francis @Pontifex • 2 September 2013

War never again! Never again war!

Pope Francis @Pontifex • 4 September 2013

Let the cry for peace ring out in all the world! #prayforpeace

Pope Francis @Pontifex • 6 September 2013

Dear young people, pray with me for peace in the world #prayforpeace

Whether it was prayer, political pressure, or coincidence, the United States delayed bombing Syria for another year.

Pope Francis @Pontifex · 10 September 2013

I thank everyone who participated in the prayer vigil and the fast for peace. #prayforpeace

Even now, at the time of this writing, Syria is hardly at peace. The civil war continues, terrorists are flooding in from the destabilized region, and while the country no longer dominates the headlines, people still suffer. So some question the pope's decision to lead an international campaign against military action in Syria. Perhaps pacifism was the wrong approach given the prolonged suffering of the Syrian people, critics argue. And with conflict hot spots continuing to pop up around the world, many involving Christian minorities suffering at the hands of extremists, Francis seems open to taking their criticism to heart.

On a swing through Turkey in November 2014, Francis suggested that Christian persecution at the hands of the Islamic State might fit within the Catholic Church's just war tradition, a sort of papal go-ahead for military action. But he also maintained war was not the only answer. "In reaffirming that it is licit, while always respecting international law, to stop an unjust aggressor, I wish to reiterate that the problem cannot be resolved solely through a military response," he said. Balancing issues of war and peace for a global leader is never easy, and Francis isn't immune to the pressure.

Areas that have been home to Christians for centuries could soon be left without any. There are whole parts of Iraq that will not have a single Sunday Mass celebrated for the first time in almost two thousand years. This unfortunate development has struck Francis particularly hard, and he's taken to Twitter several times to plead for peace in Iraq. Some see in the pope's Tweets hypocrisy, supporting military strikes only when Christians are at risk. (In Syria, the small Christian community was generally left alone under the Assad regime, and it could be even further destabilized if insurgent forces take power.) As Pope Francis confronts the challenges of leading a global church, including being the voice for Christians in places where living the faith puts their lives at risk, he continues to grapple with his preference for peace against the cold reality of a world engulfed in violence. But his default is always peace.

In addition to his worldwide prayer campaign against the use of force in Syria, the pope put this belief into action—and put some of his own political capital on the line—when he invited the leaders of Israel and Palestine to the Vatican in spring 2014. During a three-day visit to the Holy Land in May, Francis extended an invitation to Palestinian President Mahmoud Abbas and Israeli President Shimon Peres to join him, as well as Orthodox Patriarch Bartholomew of Constantinople, at the Vatican. No one expected immediate peace. In fact, even the pope himself acknowledged as much when he announced the gathering on his way home from the Holy Land: "This prayer meeting will not be for mediation or to find solutions. We are just meeting up to pray. Then everyone goes home." That's what happened.

With politics off the table, each of the four men took turns praying in their own way, chatted for a bit, and left the Vatican. Wars weren't solved; centuries of division weren't healed. But the event was yet another "soft power" victory for the pope. He demonstrated to the world that it's possible for people with real differences to spend time with one another without being at each other's throats. And it gave him a global platform to once again denounce war, in person and online.

 Pope Francis @Pontifex • 7 June 2014
Prayer is all-powerful. Let us use it to bring peace to the Middle East and peace to the world. #weprayforpeace

"Peace-making calls for courage, much more so than warfare," Francis said, commending those who "say yes to encounter and no to conflict; yes to negotiations and no to hostilities; yes to respect for agreements and no to acts of provocation."

Some might dismiss Francis's view on war as naive, but Francis knows full well what's at stake. As head of the Jesuits in Argentina during the 1970s so-called

Dirty War, the Argentine government led a brutal crackdown on suspected communists, which put the Catholic Church—and Francis—in a precarious situation.

Many Church leaders were close to the government, which ensured it a certain level of protection not afforded other institutions. But some priests, seeing so many suffer under the regime, sided with the poor. This made the military government suspicious. Critics contend that Catholic leaders, backed into a corner, decided to protect the institution over the people. But, some claim, it didn't stop there. The Church, they say, turned a blind eye to the military's torture and abuse of its own priests, so long as the hierarchy was left alone.

Though largely debunked at home, these charges were made anew against Cardinal Jorge Bergoglio in the days following his election as pope—this time on an international stage. His opponents said that as the then-provincial of the Argentine Jesuits, Francis tipped off the military as to the whereabouts of two Jesuits suspected of helping the rebels. This, they said, led to their arrest and torture. These stories, however unfounded, were some of the first things people learned about the new pope. Not a great first impression.

Since then, Francis has spoken of his experience as provincial. He said he was too young and inexperienced and, as a result, acted rather authoritarian and even "right-wing." It's an admittedly painful time for him to recall. Sensing that Pope Francis's entire papacy was on the line, some Argentine Jesuits came forward to say that Bergoglio's quiet diplomacy behind the scenes is what finally saved them. The rumors have been put to rest, but the experience of war in his native Argentina has stuck with Francis. It's no wonder he is so passionate about peace.

Pope Francis laments the violence, suffering, and death war brings, and he also has some sharp words for the economy of war, or the "military-industrial complex" made famous by former United States President Dwight Eisenhower in his departing address. This is hardly surprising given the pope's strong views on work, inequality, and human dignity. In a speech to an international assembly of social justice activists in October 2014, Francis suggested, "We are living in the Third World War," one bolstered by "economic systems that must make war to survive." These sectors of the economy "sacrifice man at the feet of the idol of money," without any regard for those who suffer in war's wake. "And no thought is given to hungry children in refugee camps; no thought is given to forced displacements; no thought is given to destroyed homes; no thought is given now to so many destroyed lives," he lamented.

Pulling from his Tweet from more than a year prior, Francis continued. "Today, dear sisters and brothers, the cry for peace rises in all parts of the earth, in all nations, in every heart," he said. "No more war!"

Pope Francis @Pontifex • 13 November 2014

War destroys, kills, impoverishes. Lord, give us your peace!

Pope Francis @Pontifex • 18 January 2014

Wars shatter so many lives. I think especially of children robbed of their childhood.

Detractors say that understanding Pope Francis can be complicated. They complain that he talks out of both sides of his mouth, and even that he lacks the intellectual heft of his two predecessors. When it comes to global conflict, in particular, some say the pope is naive to think that without war, Christians will survive Islamist extremism, in the Middle East and in some parts of Africa. The Holy See must get on board with Western-led military campaigns, they say. But based on his Tweets, the pope's views on war shouldn't leave anyone confused.

Some may disagree, but there's not much ambiguity there. In fact, if there's one message the pope wants the world to know when it comes to war, it's this: "War never again!" That's pretty straightforward. Francis wants us to bear the fruit Christ called us to produce and live by: peace, mercy, love, forgiveness, and grace. "Lord, give us your peace!"

When Francis Tweets about war, he's lending the power of the papacy to peace. This isn't particularly remarkable in itself; modern popes are almost always against war. He's also bringing his personal experience with war to the table, knowing firsthand the suffering it causes. Again, this isn't particularly novel, even for popes. But by bringing his voice to Twitter, Francis is able to rally Catholics to the cause directly, explaining to them why he opposes war and encouraging them to act. Never before could a pope communicate so intimately and so instantly with millions around the world. Today's technology makes that possible, and Francis is making the best use of it. That the pope favors peace isn't news, but the pope leading global anti-war efforts with just a few taps of the keyboard is certainly innovative, and surprisingly effective.

14

Immigration

POPE FRANCIS IS PASSIONATE ABOUT IMMIGRATION, AND HIS Tweets on the topic leave no room for ambiguity. Catholics are called to welcome immigrants, to advocate on their behalf. In addition to powerful mini-sermons of just 140 characters, as we've read, Francis is masterful at using symbols to convey potent messages. Immigration is no exception.

Before his election, Cardinal Jorge Bergoglio didn't have much fondness for Rome. He was turned off by the palace intrigue, the scandals that popped up on a regular basis, and the backroom politicking that had caused such a headache for his predecessor. So imagine his shock when he was elected pope. It meant exchanging his beloved bus rides to the slums of Buenos Aires for servants, chauffeurs, and papal protocol. After four months of being trapped inside the Vatican, Francis decided he needed to get away. Would he go to Castel Gandolfo, the papal retreat? Or maybe make a day trip up to Milan, the most prestigious Italian diocese outside of Rome? Of course not: this is Francis, the "people's pope."

Francis headed south, to the tiny Italian island of Lampedusa, near Sicily, a nearly four-hour flight from the Vatican. The island is merely eight square miles and has barely five thousand inhabitants. It's far from any commercial or cultural hub, notable only because of its proximity to Libya, seventy miles to the south. This makes Lampedusa a central gateway for migrants leaving Africa and the Middle East seeking better lives in the European Union. The Mediterranean Sea is the only thing separating individuals and families burdened by poverty, violence, and oppression from better and possibly more prosperous lives in Europe. This dangerous swath of sea has become one of the deadliest migration routes in the world.

Human smugglers charge aspiring immigrants thousands of dollars for entry onto ships with the promise of safe passage onto Lampedusa. Instead, they are herded onto unsafe fishing boats, which are grossly overcrowded, and set adrift on the sea. The engines of these boats often fail, and if spotted by coast guard officials, the captains sometimes flee the ships to avoid prosecution. The migrants are left alone, bobbing perilously on the rough seas. Sometimes the boats capsize. Entire families drown. Over the past two decades alone, more than twenty thousand people have lost their lives in this "graveyard of the Mediterranean."

It was against this backdrop that Francis, himself the grandson of Italian immigrants who left Italy for better opportunities in Argentina, arrived in Lampedusa. As his plane was landing in southern Italy, more than 150 Eritreans arrived on Lampedusa's shores seeking refuge. Dozens more died on the journey over.

Throughout his visit, Francis employed powerful symbolism to help make his point. The coast guard ship he used to make his way to the island was flanked by several fishing boats, similar to those that had offered false promises of hope to so many migrants. He dropped into the water a funeral wreath of yellow and gold, the colors of the Holy See.

When he arrived on the island, Francis greeted recent arrivals. Many had been housed in makeshift shelters, despite the pleas from local officials to the EU for more appropriate resources. Banners greeted the pope, reading "Welcome among the *ultimi*," an Italian term meaning someone at the very bottom of society. Vatican flags waved from battered and broken ships housed in a so-called boat cemetery, vivid reminders of the dangerous journey that has claimed the lives of so many. Standing behind an altar constructed of ship fragments, Pope Francis celebrated Mass wearing purple vestments, the color for penance, for what he called the "globalization of indifference" that had created these unsafe conditions.

This symbolism spoke volumes to Francis's compassion and his agenda to promote mercy. In just these 29 characters, "globalization of indifference" sums up a complex social phenomenon that leads to so much suffering. It's proof that Francis knows how to communicate heart-changing lessons in this modern and global format. Francis doesn't explicitly mention immigration on Twitter too frequently, but when he does, he pulls no punches about the moral nature of the debate.

 Pope Francis @Pontifex • 8 July 2013

We pray for a heart which will embrace immigrants. God will judge us upon how we have treated the most needy.

 Pope Francis @Pontifex • 14 May 2014

Let us pray for the miners who died in Turkey and for the latest victims of shipwreck in the Mediterranean.

Francis Tweets often about suffering, about our responsibility to care for those on the margins. Immigrants are clearly part of that category for this pope.

In his homily just off the tragic shores of Lampedusa, Francis said that all people, especially Christians, must "beg forgiveness for our indifference to so many of our brothers and sisters." He asked for pardon "for those who are complacent and closed amid comforts which have deadened their hearts."

The pope is attuned to the prevailing notion shared by many that suffering is inevitable, that it is something the well-off don't need to worry about. He blamed this attitude on the "culture of comfort, which makes us think only of ourselves, insensitive to the cries of other people." It's like living in soap bubbles, which "however lovely, are insubstantial," offering only "a fleeting and empty illusion that results in indifference to others."

With a slight jab at globalization, whose shortfalls Francis likes to point out to the chagrin of zealous promoters of the free market, he said, "In this globalized world, we have fallen into globalized indifference. We have become used to the suffering of others, *It doesn't affect me, it doesn't concern me, it's none of my business.*" Finally, the kicker: "Forgive us, Lord!" All of us are responsible for the deaths of those twenty thousand migrants, no matter the distance created by class, geography, or politics. It's a somber message, and immigration is one of those topics that prompts Francis to challenge his followers on Twitter.

Fighting the "globalization of indifference" has become a primary mission for this papacy, and this early homily has served as the impetus for two memorable Tweets about immigration, one that day and another, below, a few months later.

Pope Francis @Pontifex • 12 October 2013

Lord, have mercy! Too often we are blinded by our comfortable lives, and refuse to see those dying at our doorstop. #Lampedusa

Francis, the first pope from the Americas, has expanded his scope well beyond the European immigration crisis. During a March 2014 public audience in Saint Peter's Square, Francis promised ten-year-old Jersey Vargas that he would discuss a burgeoning immigration crisis on the U.S.-Mexico border with President Barack Obama during an upcoming meeting in Rome. Vargas's father was scheduled to be deported from the United States back to Mexico, and she asked the pope to bring her concerns, and those of the dozens of immigration activists with her in Rome, to the president. "I told him to pray for my family and to ask the president to stop deportation because it's separating my family," she told FOX News Latino. "He blessed me and told me he would bring this up with President Obama." But even a papal intervention did little to help the situation.

That summer, record numbers of children and young adults, fleeing violence and poverty in Central American countries such as Honduras, El Salvador, and Guatemala, sought entry into the United States. In just eight months, more than fifty thousand youths tried to enter the country. They were spurred on by a rise in murderous street gangs in their homelands as well as the mistaken notion that the United States would allow them to stay should they survive the treacherous journey. Many saw a humanitarian crisis in need of immediate action.

But in Washington, the issue was a political lightning rod. Conservative lawmakers used the crisis to push for more money for border security, while liberals pointed to it as the consequence of decades of deferred action on immigration reform. Ultimately, even with a president who had promised for years to create better opportunities for immigrants, the children were sent to detention centers and deported.

The situation was too much for Francis. He sent a letter along with his chief diplomat, Vatican Secretary of State Cardinal Pietro Parolin, to the Mexico/Holy See Colloquium on Migration and Development held in July 2014. It marked the first time Francis publicly waded into the thorny world of U.S. politics. Highlighting what he called "the tens of thousands of children who migrate alone, unaccompanied, to escape poverty and violence," Francis declared that, "as a first urgent measure, these children be welcomed and protected," lamenting that the migrants "continue to be the subject of racist and xenophobic attitudes." Francis urged Americans to go beyond even a basic welcome. "These measures, however, will not be sufficient," he wrote, "unless they are accompanied by policies that inform people about the dangers of such a journey and, above all, that promote development in their countries of origin." This is the Francis formula we're now familiar with: bring attention to a cause and then call for action to make it better. In this case, Francis wants Catholics to be more welcoming of immigrants, to pressure their representatives in government to enact policies that address the root causes of migration.

A few months later, just before Christmas, Francis again brought attention to the continuing crisis on the U.S.-Mexico border. He responded to letters from a group of teenagers working near the border in Arizona, advocates for migrants subjected to an increasingly hostile political climate. He lauded their willingness "to strive against the propagation of stereotypes, from people who only see in immigration a source of illegality, social conflict and violence," as he wrote to the group. He encouraged them to continue "to show the world a Church without borders," one that "extends to the world the culture of solidarity and care for the people and families that are affected many times by heart-rending circumstances."

Even after all his activism, on Twitter and elsewhere, Francis is among the first to acknowledge that current challenges persist and are even getting worse. Francis blasted the complacency of EU lawmakers during a November 2014 speech to the European Parliament. He slammed Europe as "elderly and haggard," adopting "policies of self-interest" that contributed to the crisis. "We cannot allow the Mediterranean to become a vast graveyard," he pleaded. Bring attention to challenging issues, and act to resolve them.

 Pope Francis @Pontifex • 11 June 2013

We must not be afraid of solidarity; rather let us make all we have and are available to God.

He is right, the problem is getting worse: In 2015 alone, more than one million migrants found their way into the EU through Italy, but received very little support once there. It seemed that ships sank each week, with death tolls increasing by the hundreds each time. In the spring of 2015, the largest migration catastrophe to date hit the region: close to 1,500 people died in a single week. Francis again pled with public officials to do something to help these people. He praised Italy for stepping up even as the EU cut resources, thanking Italians for "welcoming the numerous migrants seeking refuge at the risk of their lives." But he asked the international community to do more. "It's evident that the proportions of the phenomenon demand much greater involvement," he said. "We must not tire in our attempts to solicit a more extensive response at the European and international level."

Francis, evidenced by his Tweets and numerous statements on the issue, is a tireless advocate for policies that protect migrants. But as a pastor, he is aware that immigrants sometimes are reduced to faceless numbers. He goes out of his way to avoid falling into this trap.

In a message for the 2015 World Day of Migrants and Refugees, he spoke directly to migrants: "You have a special place in the heart of the Church, and you help her to enlarge her heart and to manifest her motherhood towards the entire human family," he wrote. "Do not lose your faith and hope!" En route to visit a Rome parish in February 2015, he made an unexpected stop to spend time with a poor community of Latin American immigrants living on the periphery. "Do you speak Spanish?" he asked the crowd. They said yes. Together they recited the Lord's Prayer in Francis's native tongue.

Despite his newfound role as a global statesman, Francis remains most comfortable being with the marginalized, accompanying them on their journeys. For Francis, that means speaking up for migrants, so often cast aside by the comfortable and complacent.

Whenever the pope Tweets about those whose dignity is in jeopardy, he's picturing families he met at Lampedusa, children looking for safety in the United States, and those whose watery graves are ignored by the rest of the world. He wants his Twitter followers to see in migrants individuals who might need a warm welcome, not problems to be dealt with by others. He hopes to awaken the world to the global plight of displaced people, and challenge nations and individuals to do more. Talking about the challenge of immigration, even Tweeting about it, isn't enough for Francis. He calls on us to act. It is hard to imagine a better example of his overall agenda for the Church and for Christians to be known as agents of mercy.

15

Service

FROM HIS FIRST WORLD YOUTH DAY IN JULY 2013, WHEN HE encouraged young people to go out into the streets and make a mess of things in their dioceses, Francis has made it clear he wants the Church to get out of its own head and serve others. All popes call Christians to engage in service. It's what Jesus taught, perhaps, even, his most basic message. What makes Francis's exhortations revolutionary are the way they challenge individual believers, and the Church as a whole, to stop being so insular, to greet the world as it is, and to serve others regardless of how messy it might seem.

Because he Tweets, Francis is able to communicate this directly to his flock, without the possibility of his words being sanitized or spun by others who don't share his ideas. Many Tweets take up this theme of serving others.

Pope Francis @Pontifex • 21 September 2013

True charity requires courage: let us overcome the fear of getting our hands dirty so as to help those in need.

Pope Francis @Pontifex • 4 June 2013

Christ leads us to go out from ourselves more and more, to give ourselves and to serve others.

Pope Francis @Pontifex • 23 August 2013

Lord, teach us to step outside ourselves. Teach us to go out into the streets and manifest your love.

Francis walks the talk when it comes to service, and how he chooses to spend Holy Thursday each year is perhaps most illustrative of his Tweets in action. The Holy Thursday services—during which priests reenact Jesus washing his disciples' feet—show that Francis is not afraid to serve even at the expense of rigid rules, and the possibility of causing a bit of scandal to others. "Love trumps fear" seems to be the message of this papacy.

For his first Holy Thursday Mass, just two weeks after his election, Francis headed to Casal del Marmo, a youth detention center located on the periphery of Rome. Among the twelve selected to participate in the ritual, which is usually reserved for priests, were two women and a Muslim. Francis explained to them why he was washing their feet. "It is the Lord's example: he is the most important, and he washes feet, because with us what is highest must be at the service of others. This is a symbol, it is a sign, right? Washing feet means: 'I am at your service.'" Francis said that as pope, as Bishop of Rome, he was called to serve others. "But," he exhorted those gathered in the prison chapel, "you, too, help one another: help one another always. In this way, by helping one another, we will do some good." It was yet another example of how we're all in this together. Francis wants us to pull our weight, no matter our lot in life.

The next year, Francis visited the Don Gnocchi Center, a home for the elderly and disabled in Rome. He greeted twelve residents, many in wheelchairs, aged sixteen to eighty-six. One was Muslim, and a few others were of African origin. These folks were truly marginalized. Because many were disabled, Francis had to bend all the way to the ground, offering personal attention to each resident, washing and drying their swollen, disfigured feet. "This is the legacy that Jesus leaves us," Francis said, stressing to everyone in attendance that Jesus lived a life of service. For this pope, it's about living a life based on how Jesus lived, which means a life of service.

Most recently, Francis visited the chapel inside Rome's Rebibbia prison on Holy Thursday in 2015. Six male inmates joined six female prisoners visiting from another facility. On the lap of one inmate sat a baby boy. One by one, Francis washed, dried, and kissed each inmate's feet, then repeated the process on the baby's little feet. Speaking without notes—which often leads to the most memorable remarks—Francis asked the inmates for their prayers. He didn't ask the inmates to reform their lives, nor to reflect on what had landed them in jail. That's not Francis's way.

The pope, whom some Catholics call the Vicar of Christ, asked prisoners—locked away and forgotten—to pray for him. "Even I need to be cleansed by the Lord," he said. "And for this, pray during Mass, so that the Lord also washes my filth . . . so that I become more slave-like in the service of people as Jesus did." While Francis was there to serve the prisoners, he demonstrated that even those with very little still have something to give. He challenged his followers to step up:

 Pope Francis @Pontifex • 2 April 2015
Jesus washes the feet of the Apostles. Are we ready to serve others like this?

Just as mercy is at the heart of Pope Francis's agenda, service is his primary means for embodying his message. Service can even act as a trump card for the pope. He actually broke Church law in all three Holy Thursday Masses. The foot washing ceremony is supposed to be reserved for men, since Jesus washed the feet of his twelve apostles. And it's not supposed to be open to anyone outside the Catholic faith, certainly not Muslims. (Still, since he is head of the Catholic Church, don't expect a canonical trial anytime soon.) This doesn't matter to Pope Francis. He's said repeatedly that he wants the Church to strive to be a "field hospital," healing wounds first and asking questions later.

When he washed the feet of the most marginalized— the elderly, the disabled, prisoners, ethnic and religious minorities, babies—Francis was acting as a doctor, not an insurance administrator. Whether or not the patient was eligible for the procedure could be worked out later. What mattered most was that it got done.

The pope's insistence on service has twin aims. First, in his efforts to make the Church better reflect the ways of Jesus, it is hard to argue with Francis's emphasis on service, since this so fully characterized what Jesus did and taught. Jesus said Christians must serve one another, and the pope's job is to promote the Gospel. But secondly, Francis believes serving others takes our minds off petty things like gossip, careerism, infighting, and the other maladies that accompany self-centeredness. In other words, service is a good and a cure, a preventative medicine to fight off spiritual ailments.

Pope Francis @Pontifex • 16 July 2013

Prayer, humility, and charity toward all are essential in the Christian life: they are the way to holiness.

Pope Francis @Pontifex • 21 August 2013

An excellent program for our lives: the Beatitudes and Matthew Chapter 25.

As a reformer, Francis desires his followers to be focused on building up God's Kingdom, not tearing down one another. Service is the perfect way to transform negative energy into something more positive. This medicinal use of service works at the highest levels of the Church as well as in our families, parishes, and dioceses. That's why the pope Tweets about service, and it's why he began his own papal reign with a reflection on service. Francis's emphasis on service is meant to transform both the institution he leads as well as individual believers who read his messages.

Pope Francis @Pontifex • 17 September 2013

There are many people in need in today's world. Am I self-absorbed in my own concerns or am I aware of those who need help?

Because Christ handed to Peter the keys to the kingdom, Francis, his successor, wields spiritual authority and power. But the pope is the first to say that this power is not the kind wielded by kings and queens, presidents and prime ministers. In his inaugural homily in March 2013, speaking to a crowd that included all those sorts of powerful figures—including the vice president of the United States, the German chancellor, and the president of his native Argentina, with whom he has sparred over a range of political issues while he was Archbishop of Buenos Aires—Francis elaborated on what papal power means today: "Let us never forget that authentic power is service," he said. "The pope, too, when exercising power, must enter ever more fully into that service, which has its radiant culmination on the cross."

Eschewing the miter worn by his predecessors, a headpiece signifying the power of the papal office, Francis said during that inaugural homily that the pope must "open his arms to protect all of God's people and embrace with tender affection the whole of humanity, especially the poorest, the weakest, the least important." Power is useful only when it's put at the service of others, he argued, a lesson for popes, bishops, and everyday Catholics.

 Pope Francis @Pontifex • 19 March 2013

True power is service. The Pope must serve all people, especially the poor, the weak, the vulnerable.

In a Church known for its fair share of power struggles and concern for its own prestige, a pope emphasizing and living out a radical life of service is inspiring. But it's not all smooth sailing.

The pope's global superstardom hasn't translated to a tranquil papacy in Rome. As described in the chapter on gossip, there are some in the Roman Curia not fully on board with Francis's vision for the Church, one seemingly unafraid of engaging with the world and the culture in which it lives. To say we are living through a struggle for the future of the Catholic Church isn't hyperbole; it's reality. Francis knows that. But "the struggle for power in the Church is nothing new," as he noted during a morning Mass in May 2015: "it began with Jesus."

Again, for Francis, the solution to this simmering discord lies not in political machinations but in serving one another. "There is no other way in the Church to move forward," he said. "For the Christian, getting ahead, progress, means humbling oneself. If we do not learn this Christian rule, we will never, ever be able to understand Jesus's true message on power."

For Church leaders, and all Christians, "the greatest is the one who serves most, the one who is at the service of others."

This message is paradoxical. We usually see powerful people being served, not serving others. But this paradox is a key part of the Christian message, one that Francis hammers away in word, act, deed, and Tweet, in order to encourage his followers to act accordingly.

Pope Francis @Pontifex • 17 January 2015

We who are Christians, members of God's family, are called to go out to the needy and to serve them.

Pope Francis @Pontifex • 24 January 2015

Practicing charity is the best way to evangelize.

Pope Francis @Pontifex • 3 April 2014

May we never get used to the poverty and decay around us. A Christian must act.

A Jesuit, Francis gave a special shout-out to his order's founder, Saint Ignatius of Loyola, during that inaugural homily back in March 2013. Ignatius, the sixteenth-century Spanish saint, told his followers to pray for the grace of humility. Humility, Francis said, provides the right state of mind for service.

In another homily, from July 2014, Francis noted that service is freedom, celebrating "the freedom to adore God, to serve God and to serve him even in our brothers and sisters." This is another hallmark of Ignatian life, finding God in all things, especially through loving God by loving our neighbors. Francis reminds us that we, as Christians, are called to serve others. There's simply no getting around that.

But service can't be something we do for prestige or reward; it mustn't be a photo op or resume builder. Instead, service has to be an authentic way of living. As Francis put it more memorably in an April 2015 homily: "To be Christian isn't about appearances or social conduct. It isn't putting a bit of makeup on the soul so that it's a little more beautiful." Rather, it's marked by a relentless focus on serving others, which helps us avoid the "sin" of self-centeredness. "Do I have others serve me, do I take advantage of others, the community, the parish, my family, my friends, or do I serve?" he asked. We all need assistance now and then, but we all must give something back, too. But what?

Discerning how we might best serve others is particularly important for Christians, Francis said in an October 2014 homily. The Holy Spirit gives each of us certain charisms, or gifts, and we're called to cultivate those skills so they can be used to serve others. These "rich and varied" gifts are "meant to serve the building up of the Church as a communion of faith and love," he said. He urged those listening to ask, "What charism has the Lord given me? How do I live this charism? Do I assume it with generosity, placing it at the service of all, or have I perhaps neglected and forgotten it?" Certainly some people are in need of service more than others, but Francis believes everyone is called to offer something in service. It's part of what it means to be human, to be Christian.

Pope Francis @Pontifex • 29 April 2013

How marvellous it would be if, at the end of the day, each of us could say: today I have performed an act of charity towards others!

The pope's Tweets remind his followers of this reality and exhort them to act. Francis put it simply in his 2013 World Youth Day message: "Go, do not be afraid, and serve." That's the Tweetable pope, distilling complex theological ideas to simple, memorable phrases that nonetheless pack a punch.

Francis wants us to serve because, quite simply, that's what Jesus said we should do. We shouldn't be afraid of offending by breaking a rule now and then, he says. Instead, when we see someone in need, we should step up and offer assistance. This might be contrary to what the world teaches, and even sometimes in opposition to what the Church has implied. But it's the right thing to do, as Francis consistently reminds his followers.

 Pope Francis @Pontifex • 2 June 2013

The world tells us to seek success, power and money; God tells us to seek humility, service and love.

The world may tell us one thing, but the Tweetable pope hopes we look, instead, to the Gospels.

16

Diplomacy

THE VATICAN HOUSES ITS TWITTER PROGRAM IN ITS Secretary of State's office, as we read in the first chapter, highlighting just how important the pope's Tweets have become in his effort to communicate to the world. This setup allows Pope Francis to spread his message of peace as far as possible, and in the process helps the Vatican remain a powerful voice for good. Most importantly, however, it lets Francis connect directly with his followers, free of spin, encouraging them to be diplomats at every level.

The Holy See—the diplomatic name for the tiny 109-acre nation that nonetheless wields incredible amounts of soft power—understands that Twitter can be a powerful diplomatic tool to advance the pope's message. There are no longer any barriers between the pope and his people, and he's embraced the technology that allows him to communicate his thoughts directly with Catholics. That Francis has been named Twitter's most influential global leader three years running is a sign that he and his team appreciate the potential of Twitter to change hearts and minds, and perhaps eventually, even the Church and world.

The previously unknown Francis has become a leading global diplomat, urging warring factions to lay down their arms, nations to reinvest in civil society, and individual believers to take up the cause of peace at every level. And it's not all abstract. In just a few years, Francis has some key victories under his belt. He doesn't show signs of stopping. Indeed, his activism on Twitter looks like it's just ramping up. In the chapter on war, we saw how the pope launched his #PrayForPeace hashtag in September 2013 when Syria was threatened with military action. That hashtag has continued to be one of his primary ways to communicate pleas for peace.

Pope Francis @Pontifex • 8 August 2014

Please take a moment today to pray for all those who have been forced from their homes in Iraq. #PrayForPeace

Pope Francis @Pontifex • 6 June 2014

Peace is a gift of God, but requires our efforts. Let us be people of peace in prayer and deed. #weprayforpeace

Pope Francis @Pontifex • 23 May 2013
**On the feast of Mary Help of Christians
I join the Catholics in China who trust in
the protection of Our Lady of Sheshan
and I pray for them.**

Another diplomatic victory involves the United States. In late 2014, the western hemisphere was stunned when, after decades of antagonism, the United States and Cuba announced a sort of truce, pledging to work together to reestablish diplomatic relations. The two countries hadn't had normal contact since the 1960s. A trade embargo continued to crush the Cuban economy, and as younger Cuban Americans grew up, they didn't understand why they weren't allowed to visit family and friends back in Havana. But now, a breakthrough seemed imminent.

When Presidents Barack Obama and Raúl Castro took to the airways to announce the détente, they both thanked one man: Pope Francis.

@Pontifex isn't just Francis's Twitter handle; *Pontifex* is Latin for "pope" and translates roughly as "bridge builder." And that's exactly what Francis is doing—building bridges between longtime antagonists like the hugely powerful United States and tiny Communist Cuba, just one hundred miles from Florida. He personally wrote letters to leaders of both nations, urging them to get to the table to find a way forward. So they did, meeting for close to eighteen months in Canada. The last round of talks took place at the Vatican, and on December 16, 2014, Obama and Castro spoke on the phone, agreeing to move forward. Francis latched on to this thawing in relations between the United States and Cuba as he planned part of his 2015 travel schedule, arranging for another powerful symbolic moment.

The pope set his first trip to the United States for September 2015, a three-city tour that included a first ever papal address to the United States Congress, a talk on the environment at the United Nations, and a huge public celebration of the family in Philadelphia. The hotly anticipated trip had been in the works for months when the Vatican suddenly announced an addition to the pope's itinerary: he'd stop in Cuba on his way to the States.

Though not the first pope to visit Cuba (that title goes to John Paul II, who made a stop in 1998; Benedict XVI also celebrated public Masses there in 2010), Francis's visit was remarkable because it was diplomacy in action. Like so much of what he does, the optics are the message. Francis is able to communicate profound truths without the need for dense theological reflections. A twin visit to Cuba and the United States shows the world that peace must be the path forward. The visit alone is enough to demonstrate this. A Tweet from Francis as he departed Cuba took that message right to the people.

Though the pope's visit to the wealthy United States showcased the close ties between the Holy See and Catholics there, Francis was nudging Americans not to forget the universality of their faith. By stopping in Cuba first, Francis sought to move the two nations even closer. And he might just have gained another Catholic. Raúl Castro, following a private meeting with Pope Francis in May 2015 at the Vatican, said he was so taken with the pope that he would be attending all his public celebrations in Cuba, and might just even consider joining the Catholic Church.

Though years of work remains ahead for the full normalization of relations between the two nations, the announcement of an emerging deal between the United States and Cuba signaled a third winner. Under Pope Francis, the Vatican has regained its diplomatic footing, and the Holy See is poised once again to become a major player on the world stage. Again, it's worth asking, what does Twitter have to do with secret, backroom negotiations between hostile nations?

Aside from the Swiss Guard, the pope no longer has an army to do his bidding. Instead, he relies on the Holy See's diplomatic corps—bishops and priests working around the world—to promote the Church's teaching on a range of issues. There are more than a billion Catholics, and Francis is using the latest technology to mobilize souls, so to speak, for prayers and action on a range of diplomatic issues. With just a few taps of a keypad, Francis can bring global attention to the slaughter of Christians in Africa and the plight of refugees in Turkey, and offer condolences to grieving Parisians. In the process, he achieves two major successes. His followers direct their hearts and minds outside of themselves, thinking of others while considering how they might help out. At the same time, Francis demonstrates to world powers that the Catholic Church has something to contribute to global affairs.

Pope Francis @Pontifex • 8 January 2015
#PrayersForParis

Pope Francis @Pontifex • 10 May 2014
Let us all join in prayer for the immediate release of the schoolgirls kidnapped in Nigeria. #BringBackOurGirls

The use of the #PrayForPeace, #PrayersForParis, and #BringBackOurGirls hashtags shows that Francis is willing to lend his wildly popular name and image to a range of causes. But Francis isn't just another celebrity lending his face to the movement du jour. He's seen firsthand the pain and suffering global conflicts cause, and he wants world leaders and everyday Catholics to take up these causes, too. When Francis Tweets, he's acting as a pastor to those in need, and his followers are asked to respond in kind. From local disasters to global conflict, Francis uses Twitter to communicate his desire for solidarity and mercy.

 Pope Francis @Pontifex • 18 April 2013

Please join me in praying for the victims of the explosion in Texas and their families.

 Pope Francis @Pontifex • 21 May 2014

I ask all of you to pray for the victims of the floods in Bosnia and Herzegovina, in Serbia and in other countries in the region.

 Pope Francis @Pontifex • 2 December 2014

Slaves no more. We are all brothers and sisters. #EndSlavery

 Pope Francis @Pontifex • 27 April 2013

Join me in praying for the victims of the tragedy in Dhaka, Bangladesh, that God will grant comfort and strength to their families.

A moment from the pope's May 2014 visit to the Holy Land shows his diplomatic side in action. On his way to celebrate Mass at Bethlehem's Manger Square, Francis's motorcade made an unexpected stop. Some graffiti on a security wall separating Israel and Palestine had caught the pope's attention. "Pope we need some1 to speak about Justice" was spray painted on the concrete wall in black, with "Free Palestine" written in red below. The barrier had come to symbolize the economic and security chasm between the two tracts of land.

Francis approached the wall, reached out his hand, bowed his head, and prayed silently for a few moments. Even with no words, the message was clear: the wall and its implications were sinful. Francis got back in his car and headed off to Mass. Later, the altar used during Mass was in front of a mural showing baby Jesus wrapped in a *keffiyeh*, a scarf associated with the Palestinian statehood cause.

The pope would take up the cause again the next year, when he reaffirmed the Vatican's support for Palestinian statehood and met with Palestinian president Mahmoud Abbas in May 2015. But the pope recognizes he's a global diplomat, so he doesn't align himself with just one party or cause. He calls out injustice wherever he sees it, and urges his followers to do the same.

During that same trip to Palestine, Francis visited Israel. The pope showed his concern for the plights of Jews suffering anti-Semitic attacks throughout the world, especially in Europe. In Tel Aviv, Francis put aside his prepared remarks to comment on a deadly attack against Jews that had occurred the day before, in Brussels. He called it a "criminal act of anti-Semitic hatred" and offered his prayers "for those who lost their lives." Victims of injustice anywhere have a champion in Francis, and hopefully many more who follow this pope.

Though diplomatic by nature, Francis isn't afraid to challenge his audience, in person or virtually. In fact, challenging his followers to be better Christians is one of the pope's three aims on Twitter. The pope's speech to the European Parliament is perhaps the most powerful example of the pope's willingness to challenge people to act.

Though not a European by birth, Francis, by ascending to the papacy, is automatically a power player in the European Union. He wasn't afraid to play critic during his four-hour visit to Paris in November 2014. He slammed Europe as "fearful and self-absorbed." He said that on the continent there is a "growing mistrust on the part of citizens toward institutions considered to be aloof, engaged in laying down rules perceived as insensitive to individual people, if not downright harmful." During his speech, Francis reiterated his calls for Europe to welcome migrants. Europe, he said, had lost its vigor, "a 'grandmother,' no longer fertile and vibrant." Reflect and act: the pope's mantra.

Twitter is one of the pope's most powerful diplomatic tools, as evidenced by where the operation is housed. It's also, as we've seen, his most direct link to his flock. Being the leader of a global church means being with people through all sorts of troubles.

In the past, if people were suffering through a natural disaster or man-made conflict, the pope would send a telegraph to the local bishop. These words might make their way to priests in the affected area, and, under the right circumstances, maybe the local people would hear about it. Today, Catholics in precarious situations looking for a bit of papal positivity in their lives need not wait for a telegraph (though the Vatican still sends them out). Instead, they can read the pope's thoughts, instantly, by logging on to Twitter. To cite one example, as we saw in the chapter on suffering, when Typhoon Haiyan struck Southeast Asia, killing thousands and displacing thousands more, Francis sent his condolences and mobilized Catholics to prayer and action, all on Twitter.

 Pope Francis @Pontifex • 11 November 2013

We remember the Philippines, Vietnam and the entire region hit by Typhoon Haiyan. Please be generous with prayers and concrete help.

Pope Francis @Pontifex • 18 August 2014

So many innocent people have been driven from their homes in Iraq. Lord, we pray they may go back soon.

The most important diplomatic lesson Francis offers his followers is arguably to engage with the world. It's what Jesus did, after all, even when things seemed messy and others didn't approve of his crowd. But that's diplomacy in action: focusing our compassion and mercy on particular people in need. Francis asks his followers on Twitter to serve, pray, and strive for peace. His actions show he lives by what he Tweets. He fasted and prayed against military action in Syria, he hosted heads of hostile states to pray with him at the Vatican, and he's challenged the EU to consider more just approaches to the vexing issue of immigration.

Most of Francis's followers won't ever be directly involved in high-stakes talks or in delicate matters of state. Whereas many of the pope's Tweets are aimed at bringing peace to the Holy Land or protecting minority Christian populations, our concerns seem more mundane by comparison. But the pope's Tweets about diplomacy still hold valuable lessons for us. We can use Francis's style of diplomacy—direct, fair, respectful—with coworkers, friends, and family. We shouldn't be afraid of confronting difficult situations, but we should always address them with love and a plan to act to make things right. Above all, Francis reminds us on Twitter, in every situation we should seek peace.

> **Pope Francis** @Pontifex • 3 September 2013
> **We want in our society, torn apart by divisions and conflict, that peace break out!**

> **Pope Francis** @Pontifex • 5 September 2013
> **With all my strength, I ask each party in the conflict not to close themselves in solely on their own interests. #prayforpeace**

> **Pope Francis** @Pontifex • 5 December 2013
> **Holiness doesn't mean doing extraordinary things, but doing ordinary things with love and faith.**

Revitalizing the Church means encouraging individual believers to change how they interact with the world. Is the Church under Francis becoming a global diplomatic player once again? Yes, it appears so. But the pope wants more than an amped-up foreign policy arm. He wants individual Christians to be diplomats in their own lives, transforming the world and the Church through concrete acts of mercy and compassion, one conversation, one Tweet, at a time.

Pope Francis @Pontifex • 28 April 2013

The Holy Spirit truly transforms us. With our cooperation, he also wants to transform the world we live in.

17

Jesus

ALL THE TWEETS IN *THE TWEETABLE POPE* HAVE BEEN leading up to this one chapter.

About eight months after his election, Francis re-leased *Evangelii Gaudium* (*The Joy of the Gospel*), a letter to the faithful, laying out his vision for the Church. Some have called it Francis's blueprint for his papacy. There's one sentence, in the third paragraph, that sums up his goals for the Christian community he leads: "I invite all Christians, everywhere, at this very moment, to a renewed personal encounter with Jesus Christ, or at least an openness to letting him encounter them; I ask all of you to do this unfailingly each day."

That's the invitation Francis offers the world in word, deed, and on Twitter: an invitation to encounter Jesus.

Pope Francis @Pontifex • 29 May 2014

May we enter into true friendship with Jesus, so that following him closely, we may live with and for him.

Pope Francis @Pontifex • 29 August 2013

The love of God is not something vague or generic; the love of God has a name and a face: Jesus Christ.

Pope Francis @Pontifex • 9 November 2013

Our life must be centred on what is essential, on Jesus Christ. Everything else is secondary.

There's nothing magical about the pope's use of social media. While I, and many others, certainly enjoy reading his messages, if we're being honest, his Tweets aren't particularly remarkable. Brilliant economists Tweet more persuasive posts about inequality than Francis. Peace activists leverage the Internet to organize protestors more effectively than Francis. Scientists are more adept at explaining how pollution and CO_2 harms the planet. Corporations can do far more to provide good jobs for struggling young adults than any program championed by the Holy See.

But Francis's laser-like focus on what really matters is what makes his Tweets so important. And the spotlight is on Jesus.

It is certainly not that surprising for the head of the Catholic Church, the leader of one billion Christians, to point to Jesus. What is radical about Francis, though, is how he does it. If we continually recite the historic creeds of the Church, we will say many wonderful and lofty things about Jesus ("Only Begotten Son of God, born of the Father before all ages, God from God, Light from Light . . ."), but you might notice that there is nothing in these creeds about Jesus's life, his teachings between the virgin birth and death on the cross. In other words, it's possible to worship Jesus fervently without being asked to live by his teaching and imitate his life. And that is precisely what Francis is inviting the Church to do: follow and imitate Jesus.

 Pope Francis @Pontifex • 16 May 2014

Our mission as Christians is to conform ourselves evermore to Jesus as the model of our lives.

 Pope Francis @Pontifex • 20 February 2014

Lord Jesus, make us capable of loving as you love.

Pope Francis @Pontifex • 5 July 2013

Jesus is more than a friend. He is a teacher of truth and life who shows us the way that leads to happiness.

Jesus's life, Francis reminds us on Twitter, should be a blueprint for our own. Jesus, the pope writes, identifies most strongly with the marginalized, a lesson Francis brings to life through Tweets for millions of followers. "This reminds us Christians that we are called to care for the vulnerable of the earth," he writes in *Evangelii Gaudium*.

The issues Francis highlights on Twitter, the hashtag campaigns he supports, and the 140-character homilies that appear on our feeds all have one thing in common: they point back to Jesus and offer us ideas on how to model our lives. The short but powerful messages ask us to consider, like Francis wrote in *Evangelii Gaudium*, Jesus's "way of dealing with the poor, his actions, his integrity, his simple daily acts of generosity, and finally his complete self-giving," and to arrange our lives in response.

Pope Francis spends so much time talking about poverty, life, war, evil, global events, and young adults, among other things, not because he's a political candidate seeking higher office, or a demagogue throwing red meat to his base. It's all about Jesus.

Francis himself said quite memorably that the Church's good works, its beautiful homilies and powerful speeches, and its finely tuned arguments for social justice are all worthless without a fervent belief and friendship with Jesus. "Confess Jesus," Francis said in his first homily as pope. "If we don't do that, we will be a pitiful NGO!"

Pope Francis @Pontifex • 8 February 2015

Jesus is not a figure from the past: he continues now and always to light the way for us.

That's the point of these papal Tweets. Our actions must be grounded in Jesus. Francis wants nothing more than for individual believers to draw closer to Jesus and model our lives on his. That's why Francis Tweets so much about Jesus, because without him, nothing else matters.

Pope Francis @Pontifex • 19 August 2013

We cannot be Christians part-time. If Christ is at the center of our lives, he is present in all that we do.

Pope Francis @Pontifex • 27 August 2013

Let us allow Jesus into our lives, and leave behind our selfishness, indifference and closed attitudes to others.

Pope Francis @Pontifex • 19 October 2013

To follow Jesus means putting him first, and stripping ourselves of all the things that oppress our hearts.

Every chapter in this book has been about Jesus, because every message Francis Tweets is grounded in his belief that Jesus is our friend. Francis calls us to live joyful, authentically human lives based on the life of Jesus. Nearly half the pope's Tweets explicitly mention Jesus or God, but all his Tweets point us there.

When I read through Francis's Tweets, grouping each by theme and topic, I decided that each Tweet needed a category and a subcategory. Many of the pope's Tweets deal with important topics in their own right. But Francis is clear that they are important to him, and the Church, because they are the lessons handed down from Jesus. Francis's Tweets don't point to himself, however charismatic, funny, and avuncular he may be. Rather, they all point to Jesus, challenging us to live more like him.

Pope Francis @Pontifex • 7 March 2014

Our deepest joy comes from Christ: remaining with him, walking with him, being his disciples.

Francis understands that following Jesus changes lives, and he's inviting us to join him. In *Evangelii Gaudium,* he paints a beautiful picture of how reality is changed once we encounter Jesus: "It is not the same thing to have known Jesus as not to have known him, not the same thing to walk with him as to walk blindly, not the same thing to hear his word as not to know it, and not the same thing to contemplate him, to worship him, to find our peace in him, as not to." If we respond to the pope's invitation to encounter Jesus, "life becomes richer" and "with him it is easier to find meaning in everything."

Each and every Tweet Francis publishes asks us to consider how we might live more like Jesus, to "enter fully into the fabric of society, sharing the lives of all, listening to their concerns, helping them materially and spiritually in their needs, rejoicing with those who rejoice, weeping with those who weep." When we model our lives on Jesus's, we stand "arm in arm with others, we are committed to building a new world."

Pope Francis seems like a happy guy. He exudes an infectious lightheartedness, living with an exceptionally robust vitality for a man of his age. Funnyman Stephen Colbert told *America* magazine that if he could ask Pope Francis one question, it would be, "What do you do to get that smile on your face each morning?" The answer, I think, is that Francis is filled with joy, a joy that comes from a personal relationship with Jesus. He wants that joy for us, and for that joy to permeate the Church.

Pope Francis @Pontifex • 30 January 2014
I cannot imagine a Christian who does not know how to smile. May we joyfully witness to our faith.

Pope Francis @Pontifex • 12 December 2013
We cannot think of a Church without joy. This is the joy of the Church: announcing to all the name of Jesus.

Though living the teachings of Jesus will ultimately bring us joy, Francis knows it won't always be easy, or even pleasant. "Jesus wants us to touch human misery, to touch the suffering flesh of others," he writes in *Evangelii Gaudium*. "He hopes that we will stop looking for those personal or communal niches which shelter us from the maelstrom of human misfortune and instead enter into the reality of other people's lives and know the power of tenderness." Doing this, Francis continues, makes our own lives "wonderfully complicated and we experience intensely what it is to be a people, to be part of a people." Part of Francis's mission on Twitter is to encourage his followers when things get rough. The pope doesn't want us to avoid those situations that are difficult to encounter. It's there where we might find God.

In a homily in May 2014, Francis reflected on the essential role of prayer for Christians. He described three "doors" Christians must open in order to know Jesus: prayer, celebration, and imitating Jesus. He unpacked this last point. "How must I imitate him?" we might ask ourselves. Francis answered his own question: "Do you really not remember! The reason is because the Book of the Gospel is full of dust as it's never opened! Take the Book of the Gospel, open it and you will discover how to imitate Jesus!" Straightforward and simple advice for joyful and fulfilling lives. There's certainly no dust accumulating on the pope's Tweets.

Pope Francis @Pontifex • 4 February 2014

Dear young people, Jesus gives us life, life in abundance. If we are close to him we will have joy in our hearts and a smile on our face.

Pope Francis @Pontifex • 16 February 2015

Jesus came to bring joy to everyone in every age.

Pope Francis @Pontifex • 25 December 2014

With Jesus there is true joy.

Following and imitating Jesus is what this pope is all about. Dusting off and opening up the Gospel is one way to help us make sure we're doing just that. Another tool, as I hope I've shown, is the pope's own Twitter account. From here, the teachings of Jesus arrive digitally to each of us, 140 characters at a time, straight from the heart of a shepherd who cares so deeply for his flock.

18

Francis's Invitation

A REPORTER FROM *LA VOZ DEL PUEBLO*, A NEWSPAPER IN Argentina, asked Pope Francis in May 2015 how he wished to be remembered. Francis replied, "a good person who tried to do good. I cannot ask for anything more than that."

Answers like that are what make me so fascinated by Pope Francis, and they were the driving force behind my decision to write this book. Even in the first few minutes of his papacy, Francis reached out directly to his flock, instantly becoming the "people's pope." He stepped out on the balcony overlooking Saint Peter's Square, wearing a simple white cassock, eschewing the fancy garb preferred by his predecessors, and asked for prayers from those assembled below. Only after that did he offer them his blessing. He wished the crowd a good night and told them to sleep well. The man who was just elevated to the most exalted office in the Catholic Church touched the hearts of the most ordinary of believers, making us feel like we had a friend in Rome.

Though his humility, authenticity, and charity attract attention, it is Francis's ability to connect with everyday people that sustains the popularity of this papacy and gives him this opportunity to revitalize the Church.

As we've seen, one of the most innovative ways Francis connects directly with his flock is through his revolutionary use of Twitter. With just a few keystrokes, Francis is changing the Church right before our eyes. We're witnessing a true pastoral revolution. As my colleague John L. Allen Jr. writes in *The Francis Miracle,* "By pushing Catholicism toward more generous modes of pastoral application, Pope Francis can change the Church significantly without altering a single comma in the catechism." With his straightforward, concise messages delivered a few times each week, Francis issues an invitation for us to be his allies in this mission. Together, he wants to reinvigorate the life of the Church and reorient the world toward justice.

My hope is that this book prompts you to check out Francis's Tweets on your own. Take a second to look for themes yourself, and consider how his micro-homilies might make a difference in your own life. Pope Francis's Tweets cover an even broader range of topics than I could cover here. His messages never stop surprising. You might find yourself attracted to his Tweets about Mary, the family, sacraments, hope, faith, or love. Or maybe you'll discover something else entirely. The point is Francis's Tweets have the power to reach you in surprising and inspiring ways.

Pope Francis @Pontifex • 24 February 2014

Our Lady is always close to us, especially when we feel the weight of life with all its problems.

Pope Francis @Pontifex • 9 May 2014

Holiness means giving ourselves in sacrifice every day. And so married life is a tremendous path to sanctity!

Pope Francis @Pontifex • 22 April 2013

Each one of us longs for love, for truth, for life—and Jesus is all of these things in abundance!

Pope Francis @Pontifex • 9 August 2013

We are all jars of clay, fragile and poor, yet we carry within us an immense treasure.

Pope Francis @Pontifex • 24 April 2013

Let us keep the flame of faith alive through prayer and the sacraments: let us make sure we do not forget God.

Pope Francis @Pontifex • 14 December 2013

This is Christian hope: that the future is in God's hands.

Francis wants the Church to be where God's people are, and many of us are on Twitter. So it's there that he provides short bursts of prayer, inspiration, calls to action, and even the occasional challenge. His Tweets aim to convert hearts and minds. His 21 million followers are invited to respond, and the tens of millions of others who encounter his Tweets through re-Tweeting are invited to be part of this conversation. Like the seemingly miniscule mustard seed that blossoms into a great big tree, just 140 characters have the potential to do so much more than we might think at first glance.

Saint Ignatius of Loyola, the founder of the Jesuits, asked his friend Saint Francis Xavier to travel to India for missionary work in 1541. Knowing that the journey would be difficult, and that the two were unlikely to reunite again, Ignatius sent Francis off with these simple words: *ite inflammate omnia*. Go, set the world on fire.

Nearly five hundred years later, Pope Francis, another Jesuit, was in Rio de Janeiro, speaking to tens of thousands of young Catholics during a special Mass at World Youth Day. He had one simple message for those listening. "I want a mess," he said. "I want to see the Church get closer to the people." Get out there. Set the world on fire.

In that same interview with the Argentine newspaper, Francis lamented that he can't leave the Vatican, enjoy a meal at a pizzeria, and walk alongside his people. Security and protocol prevent this, he acknowledged. But because of his embrace of Twitter, Francis is closer to more people than any other pope in history. Will we accept this remarkable invitation, to walk alongside Francis, bringing new life to this ancient institution?

Author's Note

Quotes from Pope Francis's public statements and homilies are taken from documents published on the Vatican's website, www.vatican.va. When quoting interviews given by Pope Francis, the name of the publication is cited in the text.

Acknowledgments

The opportunity to write *The Tweetable Pope* has been the highlight of my young career, and its completion owes so much to so many.

Even while managing a grueling intern year at Northwestern Memorial Hospital, Matthew Klein provided continual affirmation and assistance, reading seemingly endless drafts of each chapter, and giving thoughtful, invaluable insight and unconditional support along the way.

My family has been unyieldingly supportive, encouraging, and creative. My parents, James and Nancy, and my sisters, Megan and Kathryn, generously gave up time from their own busy days to read drafts and give feedback. And my grandmother, Helen Kroesser, listened patiently as I came up with a coherent explanation of Twitter for those unfamiliar with Tweeting.

Many individuals have encouraged me professionally over the years and they have given me a boost when I needed it most. I'm fortunate that many of these folks have become close friends. Among them is Rev. James Martin, SJ, a valued confidant who's been exceedingly encouraging from day one of my internship at *America* back in 2009. Kerry Robinson introduced me to a wide swath of American Catholicism, beginning when I was a young grad student, and her optimism and sense of possibility continue to inspire me. Alexia Kelley is, simply, the best mentor one could ask for. She's helped me navigate my way through Catholic Washington and adjust to exciting professional and personal changes, and she never fails to make me laugh with her superb sense of humor.

I am fortunate to work at *Crux* with the most talented, dedicated, and supportive journalists imaginable. My editor, Teresa Hanafin, helped fulfill my dream of covering the Catholic Church, for which I will be forever grateful. John L. Allen Jr. and Inés San Martín have welcomed me to Rome during my reporting trips there, and they continually provide me with the best insight available about the quirks of covering the Church. Christina Reinwald selflessly spent several weekends reading drafts of this book, and her expansive knowledge of even the most obscure memes and social trends undoubtedly strengthened this book.

The Tweetable Pope would have remained just an idea without the skillful guidance of my literary agent,

Roger Freet, and the superb editing of Mickey Maudlin and Miles Doyle and the entire team at HarperOne. Their willingness to listen respectfully to this first-time author's many questions—and also to provide expert answers—is greatly appreciated.

My friends have listened patiently as I explained the book's concept, they've given me their ideas and thoughts on the theme, and, most importantly, they've provided me an avenue to step away from writing when I needed a break. It's impossible to name everyone, but those who stand out include Samantha Calhoun; Carolyn Tracey; Christine Patronick; Kevin Watson; Maddy McMahon; Colin Pio; Rev. Jonathan DeFelice, OSB; Katie McKenna; Elizabeth Dias; Joshua Kaplan; Kevin Buckley; and Rev. Luigi Gioia, OSB. Dell Miller, even in the midst of seemingly insurmountable personal obstacles, always offered a word of encouragement, complete with his contagious, joyful optimism.

I'd also like to express my gratitude to Pope Francis, who has made covering the Catholic Church exciting, inspiring, and at times, pleasantly surprising. *Ad multos annos!*

Everyone listed above, and many more, not only helped make this book possible, they made writing it a lot of fun. Thank you.